Contents

Preface

Since the seminal declaration of the Second Vatican Council on the relation of the Church to non-Christian religions, *Nostra Aetate*, in 1965, the Christian churches have been engaged in a continuing and deepening reflection on their relationship with the Jewish people and with Judaism. To date, however, there has been no one statement setting out where the Church of England stands in this relationship. The document *Sharing One Hope?*, published by the then Board of Mission in 2001, marked out much of the territory to be covered, but its exploratory status was clearly expressed in its self-description as 'a contribution to a continuing debate'.

When it was suggested that the Church of England's Faith and Order Commission should produce a study of Christian–Jewish relations in order to fill this gap, the task at first appeared relatively straightforward. As a body responsible for theology, not interfaith relations, the Commission would focus on clarifying the theological positions arising from the Church of England's engagement in Christian–Jewish relations since the watershed of the 1960s. Drawing on existing texts from the Church of England and from bodies in which it is involved (such as the Lambeth Conference), the document would serve as a useful summary of what has already been established.

It quickly became apparent, however, that this project could not be confined in such tight parameters. Identifying with confidence what the Church of England has said about Christian–Jewish relations is made more challenging by the absence of specific statements carrying the authority of the House of Bishops or the General Synod. Much in this area hinges on the interpretation of the history of interaction between Christianity and Judaism; in such matters, there is seldom if ever an untroubled consensus either among scholars or more widely in the Church. Furthermore, while work on this document was underway, the renewed prominence within British public life of concerns about antisemitism, and arguments about the meaning of 'Zionism', were reminders that attempts by others to comment on the significance of the Jewish people retain a particular power to damage and divide.

At the same time, work on the project also affirmed the pivotal significance for Christian theology and practice of the Church's understanding of Christian–Jewish relations. Assumptions about Judaism and Jewish people, past and present, colour Christian approaches to preaching, teaching, evangelism, catechesis, worship, devotion and art, whether or not Christian communities are conscious of their Jewish neighbours, near and far; teasing out those assumptions and exploring them theologically is therefore a challenge that pertains to the whole Church. That challenge is also, however, a precious opportunity. As the first 'principle' underpinning this report states, we are convinced that 'the Christian–Jewish relationship is a gift of God to the Church, which is to be received with care, respect and gratitude, so that we may learn more fully about God's purposes for us and all the world.'

We hope, therefore, this document from the Faith and Order Commission will be read widely within the Church of England and beyond, including the Jewish community. We hope it will encourage careful theological thinking about the way Christians teach and preach on Scripture, and about the choices they make with songs, hymns, prayers and visual images for public worship. We hope it will raise awareness of the theological questions that should arise for Christians when engaging with debates about Israel and Palestine, as they are more or less bound to do at some point. And we hope it will encourage Christians to be confident in venturing into dialogue with Jewish people about God's purposes for us, in challenging antisemitism, and in working together for the common good of our society. We are deeply appreciative of Chief Rabbi Ephraim Mirvis's willingness to contribute an Afterword, thereby helping to model such dialogue and collaboration within the pages of this text.

The Faith and Order Commission was conscious from the outset that it would need expertise for this project from beyond its membership. We are therefore very grateful to Philip Alexander, Clare Amos, Kat Brealey, Jane Clements, Richard Sudworth and Guy Wilkinson for agreeing to form a drafting group for the document, which was chaired by the Bishop of Lichfield, one of the episcopal members of the Commission, and supported by its Secretary, Jeremy Worthen. The final content remains the responsibility of the Commission itself. It emerged from a process of discussion and deliberation, in which all involved might regret the loss of something they would have liked to see included. Our aim, however, was to produce a text that reflects the teaching of the Church of England on these matters, maps the territory of views likely to be found among its members and identifies some of the critical questions that arise from that. While this aim is more expansive than the original conception, we trust our work remains offered in humility before God.

The Rt Revd Dr Christopher Cocksworth
Bishop of Coventry
Chair, Faith and Order Commission

Foreword

By Archbishop Justin Welby

As Christians, our understanding of the revelation of God in Christ is impoverished when we fail to appreciate God's calling of and upon the Jewish people. In simple terms, the Church is being less than its true self when it refuses the gift of Christian–Jewish encounter. As such, I am delighted that the Faith and Order Commission have produced a teaching document to synthesize and resource the Church of England's theology on Christian–Jewish relations.

Understanding the relationship between Christianity and Judaism is not an optional extra, but a vital component of Christian formation and discipleship. It informs our daily Bible reading, prayer and worship, as well as our relationships with Jewish neighbours, friends and colleagues. My hope is that *God's Unfailing Word* will also impact the teaching, preaching and liturgies of Church of England congregations. At clergy and lay levels of leadership, I believe we still have much to learn about a more truthful and faithful presentation of the gift of Christian–Jewish encounter.

I am privileged to be a President of the Council of Christians and Jews (CCJ), an organization founded by my predecessor Archbishop William Temple and Chief Rabbi William H. Hertz in the dark days of the Second World War. It is a joy to see how CCJ's work today brings together Christians and Jews in a spirit of mutuality. In large part this has been made possible by *Nostra Aetate*'s reframing of the Christian–Jewish encounter, which Bishop Christopher's Preface rightly highlights. Together with Chief Rabbi Ephraim Mirvis, I have sought to encourage reciprocal relationships through the 'In Good Faith' initiative, which brings together priests and rabbis for dialogue and collaboration. Given the kindness, wisdom and scholarship of the Chief Rabbi, to count him among my friends is one of my greatest privileges. Both the warm relationship between his family and mine, and the work of CCJ and In Good Faith, are testament to the remarkable progress in Christian–Jewish relations over the last fifty years. These things are to be treasured and celebrated.

The shift that has taken place is most vividly epitomized in the symbolism of the statue 'Synagoga and Ecclesia in our Time' outside the Institute for Catholic–Jewish Relations at St Joseph's University in the United States; a photograph of this is on the cover. The image reimagines the relationship between Judaism and Christianity as one of mutual affection and interdependence. Yet only by looking back and recognizing our failures as Christians can we begin to move forward with authenticity. Too often in history the Church has been responsible for and colluded in antisemitism – and the fact that antisemitic language and attacks are on the rise across the UK and Europe means we cannot be complacent. I reflected on this as I stood alongside other Christian leaders in ankle-deep snow within the camp of Birkenau in 2016, amid the ruins of the gas chambers. The leader of our visit called on us to hear the voices of the millions murdered in that place – the vast majority of whom were Jewish. The bitter cold and the colourless outline of the landscape reflected the horror in our spirits, minds and hearts, that this had taken place and Christians had done much of it. in light of this, I welcome the way that God's Unfailing Word is unflinching in rejecting Christian failings, while hopeful in signalling the rich promise of Christian–Jewish encounter.

That said, there remain many difficult, contested areas to Christian–Jewish theology and few definitive answers! Instead, the word 'mystery' will become familiar to readers of *God's Unfailing Word* and necessarily so. The Christian–Jewish encounter raises questions of salvation, monotheism, trinitarianism and covenant. The Christian conviction that God has been revealed in the life, death and resurrection of the first-century Jewish rabbi, Jesus, rubs up against Jewish accusations of idolatry and the apparent elusiveness of the Messianic era of peace and justice. Christianity's relationship to Judaism is marked by both continuities and discontinuities – a tension which is not easily resolved. Yet within this paradox of intimacy and strangeness, we receive the gift of God.

Chief Rabbi Mirvis has done Anglican Christians a great service by writing an Afterword that reflects his misgivings over one of the 'critical issues' this document explores: the question of mission and evangelism. His words are written as a friend, and they are received in a similar spirit, however tough they are to read. As a result, I take the challenge of his Afterword with immense seriousness. To share the hope of salvation within us, a hope coming from Jesus Christ, is core to what Christians do, but we are told to do so with gentleness and grace. Any sense that we target Jewish people must carry the weight of that history. The Chief Rabbi has opened, with characteristic honesty and affection, a challenge upon which we must reflect. We cannot do that reflection honestly until we have felt the cruelty of our history.

What even this brief exchange with the Chief Rabbi highlights is that the work of Christian–Jewish relations is not finished, and that this teaching document should spur us towards more and deeper encounters where we can hear and understand each other. *God's Unfailing Word* reminds us that the diversity of contemporary Judaism, the community of lived traditions, is often very different to that presumed by Christians. The text of this document will ultimately have to be judged by the extent to which it resources neighbourly engagements between Christians and Jews in all their rich diversity; that the theological would become practical. Jews and Christians share a belief that we are all made in the image of the one God, a God of covenant, and the hope of the whole world. May God be glorified in our relationship!

✠ JUSTIN CANTUAR

The Most Revd and Rt Hon. Justin Welby

Archbishop of Canterbury

Introduction

The Christian–Jewish relationship is one of unique significance for the Church, for reasons that are explored in the chapters that follow. At root, that unique significance is theological: it concerns what is communicated about God through this relationship, and what God is saying to us through it. Hence the Christian–Jewish relationship calls for theological thinking on the part of the Church, as it seeks to recognize and respond to God's communicative action. The Faith and Order Commission of the Church of England, in undertaking this study of the theology of Christian–Jewish relations, begins from the principle that:

● The Christian–Jewish relationship is a gift of God to the Church, which is to be received with care, respect and gratitude, so that we may learn more fully about God's purposes for us and all the world.

No such study, however, can proceed without attention to the persecution and prejudice experienced by Jewish people through history, the responsibility held by Christians for that and its persistence in the contemporary context. In a contribution to a report published in 2016, Archbishop Justin Welby likened antisemitism to a virus that may appear dormant but can all too easily be reactivated in all kinds of contexts, including churches. In commenting on the specific challenges facing the Church in seeking to eradicate it, he identified theology as a vital issue: 'It is a shameful truth that, through its theological teachings, the Church, which should have offered an antidote, compounded the spread of this virus.'[1]

Two points are being made by the Archbishop in these remarks, both of which underpin this document from the Church of England's Faith and Order Commission. The first is that the theological teachings *should* offer an antidote to antisemitism. The gospel given to the Church is good news for all. The Church's calling is to witness to Christ, who is the light of God and who reveals the love of God. There can be no overlap between the truth of this witness, which it is the task of theology to articulate, and the darkness of antisemitism. God's truth sets us free to do what is right in every part of our lives. A second key principle for this document, therefore, is that:

- Truthful thinking and right acting with regard to Christian–Jewish relations follow from 'the faith which is revealed in the Holy Scriptures and set forth in the catholic creeds and to which the historic formularies of the Church of England bear witness'.[2] They do not undermine it or dilute it.

This, however, needs to be held in balance with the other point being made in the Archbishop's speech, which is that the theological teachings of the Church have in fact 'compounded the spread of the virus' of antisemitism. The attribution of collective guilt to the Jewish people for the death of Christ and the consequent interpretation of their suffering as collective punishment sent by God is one very clear example of that. Within living memory, such ideas contributed to fostering the passive acquiescence if not positive support of many Christians in actions that led to the Holocaust. Recognition on the part of the Church that it bears a considerable measure of responsibility for the spread of antisemitism demands a response from the Church. A third key principle, then, for this document is that:

- Christians have been guilty of promoting and fostering negative stereotypes of Jewish people that have contributed to grave suffering and injustice. They therefore have a duty to be alert to the continuation of such stereotyping and to resist it.

It follows from this principle that since theological ideas have been used to legitimate antisemitism, theological investigation is required regarding Christian teaching about Judaism and Christian–Jewish relations. Such theological ideas have been expressed not only in academic scholarship and in official church texts, but in everyday preaching, teaching and pastoral advice. They have been conveyed in the ways that Christians have sought to evangelize Jews, and in the ways that they have abstained from evangelizing Jews. They have been communicated through some forms of Christian interpretation of the Old Testament, and through Christian neglect of the Old Testament, as if there can be no expectation of hearing divine teaching from its pages.[3] They have been reflected in hymns and devotional poetry, in religious iconography and in ritual practices.

From these two points made in the Archbishop's speech, it is evident that there is a continuing theological task for the Church in its response to the reality of antisemitism and in seeking to build good relationships with Jewish people today. At the heart of this task is the need to outline what the Church has to say in the light of the gospel about Christian–Jewish relations. Each of the chapters that follow therefore begins by setting out some concise 'Affirmations' regarding the subject of that chapter. It is hoped that members of the Church of England will be able to use these 'Affirmations' as points of orientation, not just when they are consciously in dialogue with Jewish communities and individuals, but whenever they are touching on matters that have a bearing on how Christians view and relate to Jews. At the same time, it is recognized that there are significant questions raised here on which a wide spectrum of opinion exists within the Church of England, and indeed in some cases passionate debate. Such differences of approach to some extent mirror those across the Anglican Communion, of which the Church of England is a member, and on whose work in this area the text aims to build. A fourth principle for the writing of this document has therefore been that:

● Christian belief has a bearing on how Christians view and relate to Jews. Careful discernment is needed as to where Christians should be able to agree on clear affirmations based on that belief, where a range of positions that may be held with integrity can be identified, and where there is a responsibility to challenge views expressed by some people within the Church.

Anglican theological method is sometimes characterized in terms of its use of Scripture, tradition and reason. There are many ways to present the relationship among these three, but in what follows respect for the authority of Scripture in the life of the Church includes the expectation that the traditions of the Church and the insights of human reasoning, including historical study, will aid us in understanding its meaning. Some would add experience to these three, and it certainly needs to be constantly kept in mind that theology is work done by people and for people that is always about people, and therefore the rich texture of their lives cannot be bracketed out from this undertaking. Such experience would include encounter and dialogue with Jewish people, which may involve reflection together on Scripture, traditions and human reasoning. The significance of that experience for the development of the theology of Christian–Jewish relations underlines a fifth and final general principle:

● With regard to both resisting stereotyping and thinking theologically, Christians have a responsibility to ensure that whatever they may say about Judaism is informed by continuing dialogue with Jewish people. It is important to listen carefully and with discernment to the range of voices of Jewish people themselves.[4]

The Church's responsibility to speak truthfully and rightly regarding Christian–Jewish relations means it must also reflect carefully on the legacy of the past. For Anglicans, such reflection needs to include particular attention to the involvement of their forebears in that history. In some cases, the use of theological ideas by church leaders to stir up hostility towards Jewish communities is painfully apparent, as reviewed in the first chapter below. Yet there are also current areas of teaching and practice, such as those discussed in Chapters 3 and 4, where Christians may be startled to learn that sharp questions have been asked in Christian–Jewish dialogue about collusion with promotion of negative stereotyping of Jews and Judaism. Coming to a clear judgement on such matters is not always straightforward. Moreover, even if it is agreed that, for instance, a particular prayer or hymn has been or might be used in a way that is wrong, there may still be scope for debate as to whether it should be simply excised from public worship, or whether the need is rather for adaptation, or better education, or some combination of both. Nonetheless, the call to repentance means that consideration needs to be given to what it might mean to 'turn away from sin and be faithful to Christ' in this area of the Church's life.

These are not new questions for the churches in general, or for the Church of England in particular. In 1942, the Archbishop of Canterbury and the Chief Rabbi of the United Hebrew Congregations of the Commonwealth, together with others, formed the Council of Christians and Jews (CCJ); one of its four aims was 'to promote mutual understanding and goodwill between Christians and Jews in all sections of the community, especially in connection with problems arising from conditions created by the war'.[5] CCJ actively continues in this mission today alongside numerous additional initiatives, joint statements and actions challenging antisemitism and promoting mutual understanding.[6]

There are a number of significant resources for an Anglican theology of Christian–Jewish relations. The 1988 Lambeth Conference in Resolution 21 'commended for study' the report *Jews, Christians and Muslims: The Way of Dialogue*, which observed that 'a right understanding of the relationship with Judaism is ... fundamental to Christianity's own self-understanding', adding that Anglicans should reject any view of Judaism which sees it as 'a living fossil, simply superseded by Christianity'.[7] It is worth noting that the intention at an initial stage had been to produce guidelines on Christian–Jewish relations, but it was then decided to consider Christian–Muslim relations as well.[8] There are, however, distinctive issues in each case, which is one reason why this document focuses specifically on Christian–Jewish relations, while also being conscious of the vital importance of relationships with Muslims for Christians as indeed for Jews. Understanding the unique character of the Christian–Jewish relationship is a particular focus for Chapter 2 of the current document.

In 1994, *Christians and Jews: A New Way of Thinking* was published by the Churches' Commission for Inter Faith Relations, a Commission of Churches Together in Britain and Ireland, of which the Church of England is a leading member. It claimed that 'our own age is undoubtedly a time for Christians to look again for a new relationship with our Jewish brothers and sisters. This must involve repentance, for we are rightly reminded of the burden of responsibility the Christian tradition bears for its teaching of contempt over the ages.'[9]

In 2001, the Inter Faith Consultative Group of the Archbishops' Council produced for the Church of England *Sharing One Hope?*, a text which stressed the need to repudiate antisemitism, to recognize the continuing vitality of Judaism, to educate the Church better about the Jewish roots of Christianity and to seek opportunities for dialogue and partnership with Jewish people. It noted that it had 'no authority other than that of an occasional paper published to summarize the issues, to encourage discussion, and to suggest ways of promoting good practice within the Church of England'. The modesty of scope of this undertaking was perhaps reflected in the question mark at the end of the main title.[10]

The Network for Inter Faith Concerns has had an important role in encouraging dialogue and reflection across the Anglican Communion. In 2008, it published *Generous Love*, setting out an Anglican theological approach to relations between Christianity and other religions.[11] In 2014, it supported the publication of another report with a question mark in its title, *Land of Promise?*[12] While the catalyst for this work was discussion within the Anglican Communion about 'Christian Zionism' as a form of teaching within the Church, it quickly became apparent that responding theologically to the issues raised would involve careful engagement with Christian–Jewish relations. For instance, it is difficult to separate questions about whether God's promise of the land to the descendants of Abraham still stands from questions about how Christians understand God's promises to the people of Israel in the Old Testament as a whole to be relevant to contemporary Judaism.

While there is a significant body of material to be drawn on, then, the Church of England has not attempted to set out in a formal way its teaching in this area, as a number of other churches have done (briefly discussed in Chapter 1 below). There is a risk that the vacuum thereby left may limit the effectiveness of future work by the Church of England in Christian–Jewish relations and undermine confidence in the progress that has been made in the past sixty years, as reviewed in Chapter 1 of this report. Moreover, antisemitism continues to be an issue in wider society and indeed is perceived by many as a growing problem, whether this relates to political parties, social media or student unions.[13] Recent events in the UK context have highlighted the capacity of antisemitism to find purchase across the political spectrum, on the left as well as on the right. Holocaust denial remains prevalent across a range of different contexts, in this country and around the world, from Internet sources to the notorious antisemitic text *The Protocols of the Elders of Zion*, which can still be found on market stalls and for sale in parts of Europe and the Middle East. In this wider context, Christians need to be aware that some Jews continue to fear that Christianity is itself, at root, irredeemably antisemitic.[14]

The Faith and Order Commission has therefore produced this text so that the Church of England is able to refer to a single document setting out a theology of Christian–Jewish relations that accords with its doctrine, building on previous work in this area in which it has been involved and learning from its ecumenical partners, including the substantial series of documents produced by the Roman Catholic Church. As noted earlier, important affirmations are distilled into statements that appear in bold at the start of each of the six main chapters. While the main text of each chapter provides the argument and evidence underpinning those affirmations, it also opens up important questions where Christians are likely to continue to disagree. Boxed sections of text at the end of each chapter give examples of how the theological issues being considered relate to practical questions about Christian life and public ministry. It is hoped that the document can be a resource for reflection and discussion in Christian communities, as well as a point of reference for those with responsibility for teaching, preaching and congregational life.

The six chapters are divided into two main parts, 'Theological Frameworks' and 'Critical Issues'. The two chapters in the first part look at the 'Difficult History' of Christian–Jewish relations, and then ask what might be the 'Distinctive Relationship' of Christianity with Judaism from the perspective of Christian theology. What is it that Christians could or should say theologically about Judaism that they would not also say about Islam, or about other faiths more generally? And what might the Christian–Jewish relationship teach us about relationships with other faiths?

The four chapters in the second part consider some of the areas where the theology of Christian–Jewish relations is likely to be directly relevant to how Christians speak, think and interact with their Jewish neighbours. Debate about the land and State of Israel is an obvious topic here, where no one can be unaware of the potential for controversy, but it is also important for Christian communities to reflect on how they worship, preach and pass on the faith, including how they view Jewish people with regard to mission and evangelism. A final chapter looks at ethical thinking and action for justice as contexts where there is potential for the distinctiveness of this relationship to foster mutual learning and practical cooperation.

In the course of this Introduction, five general principles have been highlighted as guiding the approach taken by the Faith and Order Commission in this document, based on positions shared by the Anglican Communion with other global communions. For convenience, they are listed below.

- The Christian–Jewish relationship is a gift of God to the Church, to be received with care, respect and gratitude, so that we may learn more fully about God's purposes for us and all the world.

- Truthful thinking and right acting with regard to Christian–Jewish relations follow from 'the faith which is revealed in the Holy Scriptures and set forth in the catholic creeds and to which the historic formularies of the Church of England bear witness'. They do not undermine it.

- Christians have been guilty of promoting and fostering negative stereotypes of Jewish people that have contributed to grave suffering and injustice. They have a duty to be alert to the continuation of such stereotyping and to resist it.

- Christian belief has a bearing on how Christians view and relate to Jews. Careful discernment is needed as to where Christians should be able to agree on clear affirmations based on that belief, where a range of positions that may be held with integrity can be identified, and where there is a responsibility to challenge views expressed by some people within the Church.

- With regard to both resisting stereotyping and thinking theologically, Christians have a responsibility to ensure that whatever they may say about Judaism is informed by continuing dialogue with Jewish people. It is important to listen carefully and with discernment to the range of voices of Jewish people themselves.

PART 1

Theological Frameworks

1. A Difficult History

Affirmations

Judaism has continued to be a living and developing religion over the two millennia since the emergence of Christianity. It needs to be understood in the light of this history and of its contemporary reality. Judaism is different from Christianity in fundamental ways, and appreciation for Jewish self-understanding is essential for Christian dialogue with Jewish people. Christians have in the past repeated and promoted negative stereotypes of Jewish people, thereby contributing to grave suffering and injustice. They have used Christian doctrine in order to justify and perpetuate Jewish suffering, for instance teaching that Jewish people are suffering and should suffer because they are guilty of the murder of Christ, the divine Son of God, or because they have refused to welcome the Messiah. Promotion of what has been called 'the teaching of contempt' has fostered attitudes of distrust and hostility among Christians towards their Jewish neighbours, in some cases leading to violent attacks, murder and expulsion. Repentance for the sins of the past means a commitment to walk in newness of life today and to reject such misuses of Christian doctrine.

The partings of the ways

Scholarly research, particularly since the Second World War, has done much to confirm and clarify the historical rootedness of Christianity in the diversity of first-century Judaism and the extent of the interaction between Jews and Christians in the following centuries. The study of the Dead Sea Scrolls, the Pseudepigrapha (particularly the Apocalyptic writings) and the archaeology of Palestine[15] in the Second Temple period has thrown a flood of light on Judaism in the time of Jesus.[16] It is abundantly clear that the Scriptures then current within Judaism were of paramount importance for Christian origins, and that the first generation of Christians, who were for the most part Jews or Gentiles already to some extent familiar with Judaism, read those Scriptures through the lens of the Judaism of their day. Historically speaking, Christianity grew out of the rich and varied world of late Second Temple Judaism. In origin it was one of the many forms of Judaism of its time, and it drew profoundly on the Judaism within which it originated for its understanding of God, humanity and redemption.

Scholarly research has also clarified the historical origins of Judaism as we know it today. A critical period in its development occurred after the destruction of the Temple in AD 70, when, under the leadership of prominent Pharisees, the Rabbinic movement arose. The influence of this movement among Jews in Palestine grew steadily over the following centuries. It suffered grievously during the Second Jewish War against Rome of 132–135 (the Bar Kokhba revolt), when, according to tradition, a number of leading rabbis were martyred. At the end of the war, the Emperor Hadrian attempted to erase the political identity of the Jews by banning them from Jerusalem, and refounding it as a pagan city dedicated to Jupiter (called Aelia Capitolina). Nevertheless, the Rabbinic movement survived and recovered, with Galilee emerging as one of its most significant centres. Seventy years later it produced the Mishnah in its final form, the foundation document of Rabbinic Judaism, which, together with its commentary in the Talmud, is the starting point for how it understands the Torah (the first five books of the Bible, sometimes called the Pentateuch by scholars).

This historical analysis has important implications. It suggests that Judaism as encountered today – based in synagogues rather than in the Jerusalem Temple, led by rabbis rather than priests, following the Mishnah, its commentaries, and the great law codes (such as the Shulchan Aruch) – emerged at roughly the same time as Christianity. Like Christianity, it too arose out of Second Temple Judaism. Though the classic writings of Rabbinic Judaism (the Mishnah, Talmud and the Bible commentaries known as the Midrashim) can be read with profit by Christians and recognized as works of great spiritual wisdom and power, and though they contribute indirectly to our historical understanding of Christian origins, the Judaism in which Christianity is rooted is not Rabbinic Judaism. Rather, Rabbinic Judaism and Christianity share common roots in biblical and Second Temple Judaism. Rabbinic Judaism consciously claimed continuity with traditions of Jewish teaching that were actively developing before the destruction of the Temple in AD 70 and saw itself as standing in direct succession from the Judaism of immediately preceding generations. Such a claim is not made in the same way of the Gentile-majority Church from the second century onwards.

Academic analysis has a part to play in Jewish–Christian dialogue. It challenges both sides regarding their inherited understanding of their history and origins. Traditionally, each has seen itself as the true interpreter of the Scriptures of Israel (what the Church calls the Old Testament and Judaism the Tanakh), and as representing the authentic line of development from them – as being the only legitimate successor

5

and therefore the 'true' Israel. Historical scholarship raises questions as to the basis of such claims. Dialogue would be enhanced by exploring together the challenges posed by contemporary academic research.

The process by which Judaism and Christianity emerged as theologically and institutionally separate religions (often referred to as 'the parting of the ways'), was complicated and 'messy'.[17] There was no defining, single moment when the split occurred. Roman imperial persecution may to some extent have served to accelerate community divisions. The separation happened at different times and to varying degrees in different places, across the far-flung Jewish Diaspora, which in late antiquity stretched from Spain to Persia. Nevertheless, an important turning-point occurred in the fourth century, with the political triumph of Christianity under Constantine. This resulted in the definition of Christianity and Judaism as different religions in Roman law.

The fourth century also probably witnessed the eclipse for many centuries of what is sometimes referred to as 'Jewish Christianity', that is, Jewish followers of Jesus who kept distinctive Jewish customs, such as circumcision, dietary regulations and Sabbath observance. As a form of religious practice and belief, such Jewish Christianity was rejected by Rabbinic Judaism and viewed with deep suspicion, if not outright hostility, by orthodox Christianity. Fears about the retention of Jewish customs by converts to Christianity led to the establishment of the Spanish Inquisition in 1480, which continued to investigate such cases until 1700 and burnt alive those it deemed the worst offenders. That terrible episode also, however, underlines the point that the Church has never been without Jewish members. Paul's vision of the one body of Christ uniting Jews and Gentiles has never been wholly eclipsed, however much it has been darkened. What has changed over the past two-hundred years, however, is that once again there are groups claiming both a Jewish and a Christian identity: embracing distinctively Christian beliefs while also practising distinctively Jewish customs, as people who publicly define themselves as Jewish believers in Jesus Christ. This is a significant development for Christianity and for Christian–Jewish dialogue, while it also raises many questions that lie outside the scope of this document.[18]

Since at least the fourth century, Christianity and Judaism have been separated religions, which have, to a significant degree, defined themselves over against each other. Each has its own distinctive theological world view (though there are important overlaps, for example, in eschatology), its own authoritative texts (though again with an important shared element – the Old Testament/Tanakh), its own places of worship (church and synagogue), its own festivals and religious practices (though again with parallels, for example Easter and Pesach: confirmation and bar/bat mitzvah), its own prayers and liturgies (though with extensive, shared use of the psalms), its own leadership (priest/Minister and rabbi), its own symbols (for example, cross and menorah/Magen David). There are many parallels between the two, but none of them are exact or straightforward, and it is easy to be misled by apparently common vocabulary. The way that the concepts of election, covenant and salvation are used in Christianity and Judaism, for instance, has some crucial differences, and failure to appreciate that is bound to lead to misunderstanding.

As the following sections of the chapter show, relationships between the two traditions have been fraught, marred by open hostility and, from time to time, by violence. Yet there have been periods and places where relatively peaceful co-existence has been the norm. Each side continued to influence the other, for reasons that included positive appreciation as well as enduring competition and assertion of claims to sole legitimacy.[19] For example, the Sanctus, an important element of the Eucharist/Mass, probably goes back to an early form of the Synagogue Qedushah, which, like it, envisages the worshipping community on earth joining with the angels in heaven to praise and worship God. The parallels between the Sanctus and the Qedushah are even more striking in the liturgies of the Eastern Churches (for example in the Anaphoras of the Syriac tradition) than in the Latin West, where the text is rather short.

There is evidence of the influence of Christian ideas on the Jewish mystical tradition, for example on the medieval Spanish Jewish work, the Book of Splendour (the Zohar), which has profoundly shaped Jewish theology and liturgy.[20] Jewish understandings of the meaning of the sacrifice/binding of Isaac in Genesis 22 influenced Christian use of this story to interpret the death of Christ. In fact the influence was mutual: Christological readings of Genesis 22 that had drawn on Jewish tradition influenced later Jewish interpretations of the story – a neat illustration of the dialectical relationship of the two interpretative traditions.[21] The effect of encounter with Judaism on pivotal developments within Christian theology has been studied, as well as the effects on Judaism of interaction with Christianity.[22] There is a long history of Jewish and Christian scholars drawing on one another's work. The translators of the King James version of the Bible (1611) were deeply indebted to the great medieval Jewish Bible commentators Rashi, Kimchi and Ibn Ezra.[23] And it was an Anglican priest who produced the first and still widely used complete English translation of the Mishnah.[24] The exploration of these mutual and often fruitful encounters offers a positive way forward in dialogue between the two traditions.

Christianity and antisemitism

The term 'antisemitism' is a relatively recent one. It was first coined in 1860[25] and came into more common usage due to the work of Wilhelm Marr who founded a League of Antisemites in 1891. Attempted definitions are often contested. In 2016 the UK government adopted the following working definition, developed by the International Holocaust Remembrance Alliance (IHRA): 'Antisemitism is a certain perception of Jews, which may be expressed as hatred toward Jews. Rhetorical and physical manifestations of antisemitism are directed toward Jewish or non-Jewish individuals and/or their property, toward Jewish community institutions and religious facilities.'[26] The IHRA then states that 'to guide IHRA in its work, the following examples may serve as illustrations':

> Manifestations might include the targeting of the state of Israel, conceived as a Jewish collectivity. However, criticism of Israel similar to that leveled against any other country cannot be regarded as antisemitic. Antisemitism frequently charges Jews with conspiring to harm humanity, and it is often used to blame Jews for 'why things go wrong'. It is expressed in speech, writing, visual forms and action, and employs sinister stereotypes and negative character traits.

> Contemporary examples of antisemitism in public life, the media, schools, the workplace, and in the religious sphere could, taking into account the overall context, include, but are not limited to:

> ● Calling for, aiding, or justifying the killing or harming of Jews in the name of a radical ideology or an extremist view of religion.

- Making mendacious, dehumanizing, demonizing, or stereotypical allegations about Jews as such or the power of Jews as collective – such as, especially but not exclusively, the myth about a world Jewish conspiracy or of Jews controlling the media, economy, government or other societal institutions.

- Accusing Jews as a people of being responsible for real or imagined wrongdoing committed by a single Jewish person or group, or even for acts committed by non-Jews.

- Denying the fact, scope, mechanisms (e.g. gas chambers) or intentionality of the genocide of the Jewish people at the hands of National Socialist Germany and its supporters and accomplices during World War II (the Holocaust).

- Accusing the Jews as a people, or Israel as a state, of inventing or exaggerating the Holocaust.

- Accusing Jewish citizens of being more loyal to Israel, or to the alleged priorities of Jews worldwide, than to the interests of their own nations.

- Denying the Jewish people their right to self-determination, e.g., by claiming that the existence of a State of Israel is a racist endeavor.

- Applying double standards by requiring of it a behavior not expected or demanded of any other democratic nation.

- Using the symbols and images associated with classic antisemitism (e.g., claims of Jews killing Jesus or blood libel) to characterize Israel or Israelis.

- Drawing comparisons of contemporary Israeli policy to that of the Nazis.

- Holding Jews collectively responsible for actions of the state of Israel.

The Church of England's College of Bishops accepted the IHRA definition of antisemitism with its examples in September 2018, and this document of the Faith and Order Commission also affirms its value for identifying antisemitism in the contemporary context. The examples highlight the way that antisemitism tends to weave together four interconnected claims, all of which should be vigorously resisted: (a) that there is something inherently wrong with Jews as a people; (b) that Jews always seek to control and influence others; (c) that because there is something inherently wrong with Jews, this influence is inevitably to the detriment of those others; (d) that therefore those with authority have a duty to restrict so far as possible the scope for Jews to exercise any influence over others. These pernicious claims appear in secular forms of antisemitism, but it is also clear that theological ideas have been used to support them in church contexts, thereby contributing to the persistent grip of the 'virus' of antisemitism described in the comments from Archbishop Justin Welby that were cited at the beginning of the Introduction.

While the term itself appears to originate in a period of growing nationalism and racial theory, the concept of antisemitism has been referred to as 'the longest hatred', since prejudice against Jews and Judaism has been in existence since pre-Christian times.[27] For example, it was widely claimed by pagan writers in antiquity that the Jews had been driven out of Egypt, because they were lepers – a claim traced back to a history of Egypt known as the *Aegyptiaca,* written in Greek by an Egyptian priest called Manetho who lived in the third century BC.[28] The Hellenization of the Mediterranean promoted Greek society, religion and ideas as cultured; Judaism was seen as being at odds with this. The ability of antisemitism to re-emerge at different periods and in different places after apparent quiescence led to Conor Cruise O'Brien's famous description of it as 'a very light sleeper'.

The relationship between antisemitism and Christianity has been much debated. Some have argued that Christianity is at root antisemitic.[29] Some would find the seeds of Christian antisemitism within the New Testament itself, for instance in the manner in which it represents Jewish opposition to Jesus and then to the early Church, in the apparent linkage between obedience to the Law and slavery to sin and death that appears in some passages in Paul, and in the insistence of the letter to the Hebrews that the covenant given through Moses has now grown old.[30] As will be further discussed in Chapters 2 and 4 in particular, however, there are significant questions about whether such claims are supported by biblical interpretation.

The writings of some early theologians can also be cited as evidence for the deep embedding of antisemitism in Christian thought and behaviour. The surviving works of John Chrysostom from the late fourth century, for instance, include a series of homilies to Christians in Antioch written to encourage the faithful to refrain from engaging with Jews and Judaism. In strong language, Chrysostom describes synagogues as dens of iniquity and threatens those who attend them with divine judgement. That may well have included some members of his own congregation, indicating that not everyone at this point saw Christian and Jewish identities as mutually exclusive.

The modern term 'antisemitism' is used to describe prejudice against those who are ethnically or culturally Jewish, while the ostensible focus of these Christian writers was opposition to Jewish religious belief and practice, sometimes termed 'anti-Judaism'. This should have meant – and sometimes did – that Jews who converted to Christianity were fully accepted as part of the Church: the issue was not, as it was for Nazism, ethnicity. Yet there are also plenty of examples of persisting suspicion about such converts, indicating that the underlying structure of antisemitism as set out on page 11 above persisted in Christian understanding, to some extent screened and to some extent fostered by religious anti-Judaism. Concerns about 'purity of blood' in sixteenth-century Catholicism on the Iberian Peninsula, focused particularly on Jewish converts and used to limit their involvement in church and society, highlight the open border between religious anti-Judaism and racist antisemitism.[31] Expectations that secular and ecclesiastical authorities should act to control Jewish influence – if necessary with legal penalties, persecution and outright violence – also point in the same direction.

The centuries of Christian government in European history include a long catalogue of anti-Jewish measures, such as legal discrimination and periodic expulsion, alongside bouts of communal violence leading in some cases to the massacre of entire communities. Popular belief was widespread that the miserable state of the Jews, condemned to homelessness, was God's punishment for their intransigence, rejection of Christ and responsibility for his death, as highlighted in presentations of the Passion in art, drama, preaching and devotional writing. Holy Week, as a time when such narratives were at the forefront of Christian consciousness, became a time of increased likelihood of attacks against Jewish communities. As the Protestant Reformation unfolded across Western Europe, its central figure, Martin Luther, who had earlier written sympathetically about Jews, hoping that they would appreciate his reforming efforts and be converted to Christianity, came to describe them as demonic and called for the burning of synagogues.[32]

England had its own role in this history, with a claim to being the birthplace of what became known as the 'blood libel', whereby Jews were falsely accused of murdering Christian children to make Passover matzot with their blood.[33] There is some evidence of theological discussion between Christians and Jews in the twelfth century, and of concerted attempts to promote Jewish conversion to Christianity in the thirteenth. In 1290, however, England became the first country to order the entire Jewish community to leave, thereby seeking to be a Christian territory with no Jewish presence.

On the other hand, some Christians in England as elsewhere in Europe, including those in positions of authority and leadership, opposed such violent action against Jewish communities. While there will have been a variety of reasons and motivations at work, including manifestations of what may be termed 'philosemitism', there was also a recurrent assertion that Jewish survival was the will of God, and therefore protection of Jewish communities was the duty of Christian rulers. This was still regularly accompanied, however, by the idea that their punishment by God for disobedience should also be evident in their social and political status, so that they should be both protected and deprived of power, wealth and opportunity so far as possible. Here too the underlying pattern of antisemitism, with its implied duty to restrict Jewish influence (page 11 above), may be seen to recur.

Jules Isaac, who wrote on Jewish–Christian relations in the aftermath of the Second World War, saw a profound link between historic Christian anti-Judaism and the eruption of antisemitism in the twentieth century.[34] If the first premise of antisemitism is the perception that 'there is something inherently wrong with the Jews as a people', then traditional Christian teaching that the Jewish people are collectively responsible throughout time for the death of the divine Christ, and therefore guilty together of deicide, imbues it with a terrible power. Isaac coined the phrase 'the teaching of contempt' (*enseignement du mépris*) to describe what he saw as key features of Christianity's sustained hostility to Judaism from earliest times.

Regarding the Jewish people as collectively guilty of rejecting God's anointed made it natural for generations of Christians to regard Jewish suffering as divinely willed punishment. While not all Christians drew the conclusion that they had a positive duty to increase that suffering, such teaching inevitably tended to block any sense of obligation to reduce it, and to undermine simple human solidarity with Jewish neighbours. The Gospels, and in particular their Passion narratives, were, as noted above, routinely interpreted in ways that reinforced this charge of collective guilt against contemporary Jewish communities.

The relationship between 'religious' anti-Judaism and 'racist' antisemitism is a complex one. Historians and theologians may understand it in different ways, as more or less close, but there clearly is a relationship. Antisemitism emerged as a major cultural movement in Europe in the later nineteenth century, in contexts where the churches still held a dominant role politically, socially and culturally, and historic Christian anti-Judaism was undoubtedly used to give legitimation to antisemitic ideas and the attitudes and behaviour that followed from them. Christians responded in different ways – some, for instance, by seeking to make the Church more welcoming to Jewish converts, and some by supporting early moves to establish a Jewish homeland and refuge from persecution. From an early stage, a small number of Christian thinkers were deeply troubled by the rise of antisemitism and by the way it was intertwined with Christian teaching.[35] It cannot be denied, however, that these represented a minority voice at the time. The widespread embrace of antisemitism, most extremely but not solely in Nazi Germany, and the unfathomable evil of the Holocaust moved such concerns towards the mainstream of thinking in many churches in the course of the twentieth century, particularly from the 1960s.[36]

Christian theologies of Judaism in the twentieth century

In the midst of the mass persecution and murder of Jews in the 1930s and 1940s, some Christian theologians responded by affirming the continuing election of the Jewish people as part of Christian teaching. A significant contribution here was made by James Parkes, an Anglican clergyman whose work in Continental Europe during the 1920s and 1930s led to a lifelong commitment to the study of Judaism and Christian–Jewish relations as crucial for resisting antisemitism. His most important work, *The Conflict of the Church and the Synagogue*, was published as early as 1934, and both his scholarship and his campaigning greatly influenced those responsible for the establishment of the Council of Christians and Jews, referred to in the Introduction.[37]

Many of the major figures of twentieth-century theology in Europe were profoundly affected by the treatment of the Jewish people that they witnessed in this period. Bonhoeffer would perhaps be the most famous example, but one could mention from the Roman Catholic Church Maritain and de Lubac (who became involved with underground resistance activities in France against antisemitism during the Second World War) and Barth from the Reformed.[38] In lectures he gave in 1946 in Bonn, Barth asserted that the nation of Israel

> embodies in history the free grace of God for us all … If as Christians we thought that Church and Synagogue no longer affected one another, everything would be lost. And where this separation between the community and the Jewish nation has been made complete, it is the Christian community which has suffered.[39]

In the decades after 1945, many churches began searching for a new approach, struggling to reconcile an acceptance of some responsibility for the Holocaust and a desire for a new relationship with Judaism with the difficulty of revisiting long-held teachings. This can be seen in the declarations by the World Council of Churches and other church organizations at this time; the First Assembly of the World Council of Churches, meeting in Amsterdam in 1948, affirmed 'the special meaning of the Jewish people for Christian faith' and rejected antisemitism 'as absolutely irreconcilable with the profession and practice of the Christian faith' and as 'sin against God and man'.[40] Another indication of a fresh approach was the statement 'On the Jewish Question', issued by the Evangelische Kirche in Deutschland in 1950, which included the assertion that 'We believe God's promise to be valid for his chosen people even after the crucifixion of Jesus Christ.'[41] What such a theological claim might mean is discussed further below.

The establishment of the State of Israel is also relevant to these developments. It implicitly challenged traditional Christian claims that the degradation of the Jewish people and specifically their continuing exile from the land were proof of their punishment by God for failing to accept Jesus as Messiah and Lord. It created a new context for Christian–Jewish relations in Israel, in which Judaism became the majority religion and Christianity marginal. It demonstrated the continuing vitality of Judaism, even for those who disapproved of the creation of the new state as the flawed human pre-emption of divine action. Its military successes, including its incorporation of the Old City of Jerusalem following the Six-Day War in 1967, confirmed this impression for many Christians, with some wondering whether they were seeing in their own time the fulfilment of biblical prophecy.

In the mid-1960s, with the historic statement of the Second Vatican Council on the Church and other religions in 1965, known as *Nostra Aetate*, the ground was laid by the Roman Catholic Church for the explicit abandonment of the charges of collective guilt against the Jewish people for rejecting the Messiah and for deicide: 'The Jews should not be presented as rejected or accursed by God, as if this followed from the Holy Scriptures.'[42] *Nostra Aetate* distinguished between biblical and theological studies and fraternal dialogue, recommending both as the way forward. The Vatican has been faithful to that commitment in presenting a series of further declarations, notes and reflections.[43]

Other churches have also made clear since the 1960s their rejection of key aspects of the 'teaching of contempt', including the idea of collective guilt attaching to the Jewish people for the death of Christ. The Church of England shares this consensus that such ideas should have no place in

Christian teaching and belief. The then Archbishop of Canterbury, Michael Ramsey, issued a statement in 1964 in which he said: 'It is always wrong when people try to lay the blame upon the Jews for the crucifixion of Jesus Christ.'[44] Where there is less clarity, however, is on what the Church should be saying positively about Judaism as a living religion. As noted above, the Evangelische Kirche in Deutschland stated back in 1950 that 'We believe God's promise to be valid for his chosen people even after the crucifixion of Jesus Christ.' What, however, is the promise that remains 'valid' in this judgment? Does the crucifixion and resurrection of Christ change anything for God's 'chosen people', or is the gospel of Christ only relevant for others?

Scholars of Christian–Jewish relations sometimes use the term 'supersessionism' as shorthand for a flawed Christian theology that denies the continuing place of Jewish people and of Judaism as a community of faith in the purposes of God.[45] Echoing this terminology, *Jews, Christians and Muslims* 'firmly' rejected any suggestion that Judaism had been 'simply superseded' by Christianity, quoting Romans 11.29 – 'for the gracious gifts and his calling are irrevocable'.[46] Others speak of 'replacement theology', to refer to the claim that the Church has replaced (old) Israel in the purposes of God. There would, however, be different views among theologians working in this area as to how to articulate a Christian understanding of Judaism as a living reality, and indeed as to what elements in the Christian theological inheritance might be incompatible with a right understanding of Judaism and therefore need to be rejected. The next chapter will consider some of the parameters for the Church of England's approach to these important questions.

The need for repentance

Such attempts to formulate a renewed theology of Christian–Jewish relations over the past hundred years may be located in a context of ecclesial repentance for complicity with the evils of antisemitism. As is already clear in *Nostra Aetate*, wrong theology in this area has been bound up with wrong action, giving legitimation for Christian support for persecution and discrimination of Jewish communities and eroding the recognition of Jewish people as neighbours whom Christians are bound to love.

The idea of the one, holy, catholic and apostolic Church repenting for sins it has committed raises some significant questions for Christian theology.[47] Nonetheless, the concept of responsibility for sin being shared by members of a community both present and past has deep roots in Christian tradition, including the Scriptures. Where the continuing effects of past sins by members of the one body of Christ continue to be felt and where those sins have not come to an end, then members of Christ's body here and now are bound to seek God's mercy. Repentance in this as in any other context needs to identify and name what is sinful, letting it be seen for what it is in the light of God's righteousness, and not take refuge in vague generalities. It also needs to lead to a commitment to walk in newness of life, accepting disciplines of changed behaviour that follow from that. Christian communities may wish to consider whether there could be suitable opportunities in their public worship to focus and express repentance for Christian involvement in fostering antisemitism, for instance in relation to observance of Holocaust Memorial Day.

Theology and practice: how do we deal with the living legacy of anti-Judaism?

Two Church of England cathedrals, Norwich and Lincoln, were associated with the development and spread of the 'blood libel' in the later Middle Ages, which, on the basis of the death of a child, falsely accused Jewish communities of abducting and killing Christian children to use their blood in the making of Passover matzos. This allegation, originating in England, became the catalyst for the murder of many Jews in this country and across Europe, especially in pogroms at Eastertide. The tombs where the children were buried became shrines that were a focus for pilgrimage and devotion until their destruction along with other such places at the Reformation.

If you visit these cathedrals today, you will find public material that refers to these histories.

In Lincoln, the relevant sign near the tomb of the child known as Hugh concludes with these words:

> This libel against the Jews is a shameful example of religious and racial hatred, which, continuing down through the ages, violently divides many people in the present day. Let us unite, here, in a prayer for an end to bigotry, prejudice and persecution. Peace be with you: Shalom.

In Norwich, a notice at the Chapel of the Holy Innocents concludes:

> William was a 12 year old Norwich boy whose murdered body was found outside the city on Mousehold Heath in Holy Week, 1144. Members of his family accused the Jews of Norwich of killing him ... This was, however, the first recorded instance of the influential 'blood libel' against the Jews, taken up in other places around the world with murderous consequences.

This Chapel was restored to use in 1997 and dedicated in the presence of Jewish representatives as a place for remembering the sufferings of all innocent victims, particularly the young. It is also a place of prayer for reconciliation between people of different faiths, remembering especially all victims of Christian–Jewish persecution.

What would be an appropriate Christian response today to remembering what Christians have done in the past to Jewish people in these places? Would it include repentance, and, if so, how should that be expressed?

What do you think encouraged many people in the Middle Ages to believe the story about the blood libel? Are there parallels in our contemporary context?

2. A Distinctive Relationship

Affirmations

Jesus of Nazareth, whom Christians believe to be Israel's Messiah and the Saviour of the world, lived and died as a Jew in faithful service to 'the God of Abraham, Isaac and Jacob'. The Scriptures that informed and guided the life of Jesus were the books the Church now refers to as the Old Testament, having resisted at a formative stage attempts to remove them from its canon of Scripture or relegate them to an inferior status. Although there are significant differences between Christianity and Judaism in their reading of these common texts, both receive them as inspired by God, enabling the people of God to hear the word of God today. They provide for Jews and Christians common texts for worship and prayer, and sources on which they may confidently draw to address the creator of the world. While Christians have responded in different ways to Jewish self-understanding as God's people, they should neither reject it as simply mistaken nor accept it as independent from God's saving work in Jesus Christ. The relationship between Christianity and Judaism is characterized by both kinship and divergence, and the idea of Judaism as a 'sacrament of otherness' for the Church provides one way to appreciate the distinctiveness of this relationship.

Jesus, Judaism and the Scriptures

Jesus was a Jew who read the Tanakh (which Christians now call the Old Testament), and faithfully followed and interpreted for his followers the prescriptions of the Torah (Matthew 5.17 and Matthew 8.4). The first and most familiar title for Jesus with theological significance is taken from the Old Testament and expresses his significance for Israel: Christ, meaning 'anointed one', with the Hebrew equivalent usually Anglicized as 'Messiah'. While debate continues as to the understanding of this term in the context of first-century Judaism, the Church's claims about Jesus beginning from the New Testament make no sense without the calling of Israel to be God's faithful people.[48]

The New Testament is full of quotations from the Jewish Scriptures of the day, which are accepted as the word of God and quoted as divine authority.[49] In the course of the second century, the Church emphatically repudiated the view of Marcion and the Gnostics that the God of the Old Testament was different from the God of the New, and that the Jewish Scriptures should, therefore, be excluded from the Church's canon of sacred Scripture.[50] It affirmed the identity of the God of the Old Testament with the God of the New, making the Scriptures the churches knew from Judaism the basis for their canon. Ever since, the centrality of these Scriptures to the Christian Church has been given concrete expression in the Church's lectionary, in the widespread use of the psalms in Christian worship, and in Christian preaching and teaching.

Claims that there is a distinction between the Old Testament God of wrath and the New Testament God of love are contemporary forms of Marcionism and need to be resisted. Care needs to be taken that the affirmation of the unity of God's action in revelation and redemption is not undermined in other ways, such as by drawing an opposition between an old covenant of 'works' and a new covenant of 'grace', when God's covenant-making with humanity has, from the beginning, flowed from divine grace, mercy and love, calling for a human response of thankfulness that finds expression in acts of loving service. While Christians will read the Old Testament in the light of Christ, they should not see the New Testament as a rupture inconsistent with the earlier revelation.[51]

The Gospels provide evidence of debate and conflict between Jesus and other Jewish teachers and groups, while other books of the New Testament, in particular the book of Acts, show how such debate and conflict continued to be part of the experience of the early Christian movement. Inevitably, however, such accounts were liable from an early stage to be interpreted differently by Gentile Christian communities who had limited comprehension of Judaism and might themselves experience tense relationships with local Jewish communities. They could begin to be heard as indictments of Judaism and its adherents as such, rather than as descriptions of impassioned exchanges *within* Judaism arising from the startling claims made by and about the Jewish teacher, Jesus of Nazareth, by his largely Jewish followers. Challenges relating to the reading of such biblical texts in contemporary church life are addressed in Chapter 4 below.

There is a long tradition going back to the early centuries of the Church of considering the Jewish people to have a continuing role as faithful custodians of the Old Testament/Tanakh. As already noted, since the second century AD, there has been no significant dispute regarding the inclusion of the books contained in the Jewish Tanakh in the Church's Old Testament as an integral part of its Scripture. Alongside this core canon of those texts of which Judaism has preserved copies in their Hebrew and Aramaic originals, some churches also include other texts, also Jewish in origin, but not recognized by Rabbinic Judaism, which were composed originally in Greek, or which have not been preserved in their Hebrew/Aramaic originals. These texts would be seen by many Christians, including Anglicans, as having a secondary though still important status – as apocryphal or deuterocanonical.[52]

Since at least the time of Jerome, and particularly during the Reformation of the sixteenth century, Christian scholars have employed Jewish scholars to teach them Hebrew and Aramaic, and thus enable them to gain access to their Old Testament in its original languages. This debt is evident in the great classic Christian translations of the Old Testament, such as the King James Bible of 1611, and has continued down to the present day. Within the academic world a deeply fruitful dialogue and debate exists between Jewish and Christian scholars (at conferences and seminars, as well as in articles and monographs) on the meaning of the Tanakh/Old Testament in its historical context. This constitutes a valuable resource for the Church.

At the same time, it is important to recognize that in a confessional as opposed to an academic context the two religious communities approach the text from distinctive hermeneutical perspectives, in which it is read in the light of other, different texts, as well as from a different sense of who 'we' are in relation to the people and events set out in these Scriptures. For Christianity the Old Testament needs to be read alongside the New, in whose light it is understood to have a prophetic dimension throughout, as a set of texts that look forward to God's revelation in Jesus Christ. Rabbinic Judaism, on the other hand, finds the centre of gravity for the Tanakh in the Torah ('Law'), receiving it as God's teaching for life here and now, and looking for interpretative guidance to the Mishnah, a compilation of Jewish religious law traditionally ascribed to Judah ha-Nasi around AD 200, to the Talmud as a whole and to Midrash (homiletical and halakhic/legal exposition of the Tanakh). These texts and the ongoing traditions of their interpretation in turn connect the Jewish reader in the present across the generations to their forebears whose words and deeds are recounted in the biblical text. The integrity of these distinct hermeneutical approaches needs to be understood and respected; Jews and Christians share common objects of spiritual and religious attention in remarkable ways, and yet they also look at those common objects from quite different perspectives.

Describing the relationship

There is, then, a unique relationship between Christianity and Judaism bound up with their difficult history. Scholars will continue to debate various aspects of the emergence of Christianity as a religion distinct from Judaism, as set out in the previous chapter, but one cannot tell the story of how the Church came to be without talking about Judaism, not least because the drama of divergent Jewish responses to Jesus Christ is woven through the New Testament texts. Moreover, those texts affirm as Scripture the books of what Christians call the Old Testament, which they share as Scripture with Jewish people then and now, and also interpret those books in ways that most Jewish people would contest then and now. The history that shapes the identity of Christian faith, as handed down through the Scriptures of the Church, therefore sets Christianity and Judaism in an unavoidable relationship of both kinship and divergence. This is in some sense a family relationship, because the historical origin of Christianity, as of Rabbinic Judaism, lies in the diversity of first-century Judaism (see pages 3–5 above), and because the defining texts and actions of Christianity tell the story of Israel as part of the Church's story. It is also a relationship marked by the lasting effects of the 'parting of the ways' between Christianity and Judaism in the first four centuries of the Church as described in the previous chapter, a parting that cannot be explained simply in terms of failures in communication or in mutual good will. Jewish Christians and the Gentiles who joined them set out on a path that went in a different direction from the way taken by most Jews in this formative period – and yet the kinship remains.

Because of the divergence between them, Christians and Jews will have different perspectives on the kinship that also exists between them. Moreover, as noted at the end of the preceding section, the fact that they use common vocabulary drawn from overlapping canons of Scripture may obscure the contrast between the way they use and understand the same words. At this point in the document, however, it is necessary to begin to shape some central theological questions for Christians about the relationship between the Church and the Jewish people – questions that are formulated in distinctively Christian terms, yet without ceasing to be attentive to how they may sound to Jewish hearers, who will themselves have very varied perspectives.

When Christians who believe that they belong to God's chosen people through Jesus Christ become aware that Jewish people may believe that they belong to God's chosen people without him, they are bound to be aware of the apparent tension. Is it an unavoidable tension between contradictory positions, or could it be better understood as a matter of different perspectives, for example, what Christians and Jews mean by 'belonging to God's chosen people' is not the same thing and therefore the two beliefs are not in conflict? There would also be different understandings within Christianity of what might be meant by 'God's chosen people'. Still, the apparent tension between Christian and Jewish self-understanding on this point provides a useful initial point of departure for exploring different approaches within Christian theology to describing the Christian–Jewish relationship. There has been a wide variety of responses to that perceived tension in Christian history and especially over the last hundred years, as indicated in pages 16–19 of the previous chapter. While there is clearly a spectrum of views held by Christians – and not a neatly linear one either – four broad positions might be identified that would have some degree of purchase among Christians today as well as support from theologians in the past.

The first response to the apparent tension between Christian and Jewish beliefs about the people of God is an *unqualified denial* of the claim of Jewish people since the time of Christ to be part of God's chosen people. The incarnation, crucifixion and resurrection of the Son of God means that the people of God are now defined as those who receive him and believe in him. Those who do not receive him and believe in him are not part of God's people today. Israel before Christ was faithful in so far as it accepted the promises that pointed towards him and lived under the covenant given by God to prepare the way for him. Now that he has come, to hold on to the Scriptures that describe the promises now fulfilled in him and the covenant now made new through him yet without believing in him and adhering to his teaching is to place oneself outside the company of God's people. Numerous passages from pre-modern theologians could be cited as expressing this position. It might also be extended to accommodate the very different approach of some modern 'liberal' theologians such as Schleiermacher, who denied any relationship of enduring theological significance between the Church and the Jewish people, and Harnack, for whom 'Judaism' was a phase of religious development that reached its end in the first century AD with the arrival of Christianity.[53]

The second response is an *acceptance qualified with some correction* of the claims of Jewish people after the time of Christ that they are God's chosen people. It is accepted that the promise God made to Abraham and his descendants applies to all Jewish people throughout history, religious or secular, who are chosen irrevocably by God to be God's people, living under God's covenant. Yet it is also true that through Jesus Christ the covenant has been made new, and God's will is for all people to enter into the renewed covenant in Christ's blood, Jews and Gentiles alike. Jewish people therefore need to discover and respond to this divine gift as God's irrevocably chosen people. Karl Barth, also mentioned in the previous chapter, would be a representative of this position, but others could be found from much earlier in Christian history. Indeed, it might be said that the Christian tradition prior to the twentieth century has been marked by something of an unresolved ambivalence between these first two positions.

The third response is an *acknowledgement of mystery regarding* the claims of Jewish people after the time of Christ that they are God's chosen people. The Church, which has become predominantly Gentile since the generations after the apostles and carries a heavy burden of responsibility for antisemitism and its lethal consequences, as set out in the previous chapter, cannot come to a satisfactory theological judgement regarding how Jewish people since the coming of Christ nonetheless remain recipients of God's promises. It has to accept that there is a mystery here that transcends its understanding in history, though its meaning will be revealed at the end of time. It should not therefore deny the continuing relationship of covenant love between Jewish people and the one God, but neither should it deny the claims it makes on the basis of the Scriptures as summarized in the historic creeds about Jesus Christ as the Son of God incarnate and as the Saviour of the whole world. This is a position that can be found in some Roman Catholic thinkers from the last century, such as Jacques Maritain (also referred to in the previous chapter) and before him, in the nineteenth century, León Bloy. There would be some overlap between more 'affirming' versions of this kind of response and more 'questioning' versions of the previous one.

The fourth response is an *unqualified affirmation* of the claims of Jewish people after the time of Christ that they are God's chosen people. The identity of the Jewish people as God's people Israel is essentially unaffected by the incarnation, crucifixion and resurrection of the Son of God. One of the ways in which this has been expressed over the past hundred years has been to speak of two covenants: a covenant with the Jewish people through Moses, and a covenant with the Church through Jesus Christ. Both have been established by God. Both share a common root in the covenant with Abraham, and neither is ultimately independent from the other. Each can learn from the other and each should appreciate and value the other for its distinct purpose within

God's design for revelation and salvation. There are two ways of being the people of God. While this position can already be found in the writings of the Anglican thinker James Parkes in the 1930s, it becomes much more prominent as Christians begin to grapple in earnest with the impact of the Holocaust for Christian theology from the 1960s onwards. The writings of another theologian from the Anglican Communion, Paul van Buren, might be mentioned in this context. Some would see this as the only response that is truly free from the 'supersessionism' identified as the root of historic Christian anti-Judaism, which provided a fertile seed-bed for murderous antisemitism in the modern era, so that there is an ethical imperative for Christians to adopt it.

Readers of this document are likely to include Christians who would identify with each of the four responses to the initial question sketched out above. Each, as noted, can claim support from significant theological voices. Each can be argued on the basis of a reading of key passages in the New Testament. That is not to say, however, that each can be argued with equal plausibility, or that any version of any of the four responses can 'be held with integrity' (to use the wording of the fourth principle in the Introduction). Christians should also be aware that while there would be a range of views on such matters among Jewish people, many would find some or all of these responses problematic for various reasons.

Another way to frame the theological issues at stake here might be to ask: in what way do Jewish people living after God's revelation in Jesus Christ who do not receive that revelation continue to be Israel, as a living reality that the Church confesses in its worship and its teaching, not least in its naming of God as the God of Israel? The first response corresponds to a position that would say: Jewish people are not now Israel at all, because what God once gave to Israel before Christ God now gives to the Church in Christ, which has become the Israel of God. According to the second response, the Jewish people as a whole do indeed continue to share in the living reality of Israel, but in a way that is limited and indeed diminished by the absence of response to the gift of Christ. For the third, there would also be an affirmation of Jewish people's continuing participation in Israel, but a withholding of judgement as to what might limit or increase it. The fourth response would be characterized by a preference for regarding the Jewish people rather than the Church as Israel, with 'Israel' and 'Church' being seen as parallel though interrelated communities through whom God works in the world. For the first position, only the Church is Israel today; for the fourth, the Jewish people continue to be Israel, regardless of the Church. The second and third positions accept both the claim of the first that the Church is now Israel and the claim of the fourth that the Jewish people remains Israel, but they have different approaches as to how to hold these two claims together.

Romans 9–11 provides the most sustained, direct treatment in the New Testament of the question of what the lack of recognition of God's work in Christ on the part of most Jewish people means for the theological understanding of the Jewish people collectively as Israel. It is no accident that it has been the biblical passage repeatedly turned to over the past century by theologians seeking to respond to antisemitism by recovering a Christian understanding of God's purpose in and for continuing Judaism. The major section in Barth's *Church Dogmatics* on Church and Israel is an extended exposition of Romans 9–11. It also needs to be borne in mind, however, that the interpretation of Paul has been the subject of intensive debate in New Testament studies since the 1980s, and that the centre of gravity within the debate has been far from stable. Moreover, arguments about the context, purpose and key message of Paul's letter to the Romans have played a pivotal role within this academic controversy. Two of the pivotal issues here have been the extent to which Paul's thinking in general exhibits an essential coherence, and how far Romans in particular should be read as following a connected line of argument.[54]

Paul begins his discussion in Romans 9–11 with some deeply personal reflection: 'I have great sorrow and unceasing anguish in my heart. For I could wish that I myself were accursed and cut off from Christ for the sake of my own people, my kindred according to the flesh' (Romans 9.2-3). That Paul continued to regard himself as a Jew and the Jewish people as 'my own people' is evident elsewhere in his letters and indeed in the speeches attributed to him in Acts.[55] The cause of this anguish becomes clear in what follows: most Jewish people, including those whom Paul has worked tirelessly to persuade through face-to-face argument, have not received Jesus of Nazareth as Christ and Lord. At 11.11-12, he writes of their *paraptoma*, translated here by the NRSV as 'stumbling', though more usually rendered in English versions of the New Testament as 'transgression'. For Paul, God's calling of Israel is ordered towards Christ, and therefore the absence of recognition of what God has done in Christ on the part of most Jewish people is a source of great perplexity and sadness for him. The fourth response, as set out above, is evidently not Paul's response when he is writing Romans: that his Jewish brothers and sisters should receive God's gift in Christ matters profoundly to him.

To put to one side for a moment the exegesis of Romans 9–11, it is also difficult to see how versions of the fourth response that would resist affirming Jesus Christ as the Son of God made incarnate for the salvation of all, Jews and Gentiles alike, can be compatible with the teaching of the Church of England, including its upholding of the historic creeds, which teach the divinity of Christ and his saving work for all people. If it is true that the eternal Word of God has been made flesh and dwelt among us, how can this be a matter of no relevance for the people who are 'his own' (John 1.11-14)? If God the Father gave his only-begotten Son so that we might have life in all its fullness by abiding in him (John 10.10), then are Jewish people to be denied this fullness? Moreover, one might also ask whether it is possible to take this approach and regard the writings of the Old Testament as fully Christian Scripture. According to Article VII of the Church of England's Thirty-Nine Articles of Religion, 'both in the Old and the New Testament everlasting life is offered to Mankind by Christ'. The first principle from the Introduction is relevant at this point.

At the same time, however, it seems clear that Paul does affirm in Romans 9–11 that the Jewish people of his day – and therefore of ours – continue to share in some way in the reality of Israel; after all, he follows the account of his own anguish in the first two verses of Romans 9 with the affirmation: 'They are Israelites, and to them belong the adoption, the glory, the covenants, the giving of the law, the worship, and the promises; to them belong the patriarchs, and from them, according to the flesh, comes the Messiah, who is over all, God blessed forever. Amen' (Romans 9.4-5). The fundamental question that the lack of openness to the gospel within Jewish communities poses for Paul is whether the God of Israel has failed in his covenant with the Israelites, who are and remain God's elect. Paul's response to this is emphatically 'By no means!', as is made clear in the statement that immediately follows: 'It is not as though the word of God has failed' (Romans 9.6a).

Confidence in God's faithfulness, however, is certainly not the same thing as presumption as to whom God calls, as Paul then proceeds to explain. Indeed, it has been argued that the key to Paul's thought here and through the rest of the passage is the insistence that belonging to God's people is always a matter of God's gift, God's grace.[56] It can never be something derived from some other foundation (such as biological descent) or claimed as an enduring right on our part. His message on this point, writing to predominantly Gentile congregations in Rome, is primarily intended to warn them against presumption and specifically against indifference and disdain regarding the Jewish Christians who are also present there.

Hence the message in these chapters both that no claim to be 'Israel' can rest on anything other than God's gracious promise, and that God's gracious purpose for Israel, though apparently thwarted, has not been set aside by God and therefore cannot be dismissed by Gentile Christians. This emerges most clearly at the beginning of the concluding section of the passage, where Paul writes: 'So that you may not claim to be wiser than you are, brothers and sisters, I want you to understand this mystery: a hardening has come upon part of Israel, until the full number of the Gentiles has come in. And so all Israel will be saved' (Romans 11.25-26a). Part of Israel has been 'hardened' – the language used with regard to Pharaoh in Egypt is shockingly applied here to those who would see themselves as descendants of those delivered from him. Yet that part of Israel *remains* Israel, and God's purpose abides that 'all Israel will be saved', both the part that has been hardened and the part that has already received God's promise in Jesus Christ. Paul is also clear, therefore, that the Jewish people continues to share in the theological reality of being Israel, by contrast with the first response as outlined above. This was the point made forcefully by Barth and others on the basis of Romans 9–11 in responding to the extreme versions of that position being promoted by those seeking to provide Christian support for antisemitism in Nazi Germany and elsewhere.

Moreover, it is difficult to maintain the *unqualified* denial that Jewish people since the time of Christ have any share in the covenant and promises of God without either undermining confidence in the scriptural witness of the Old Testament to God's covenant-making with Abraham and his descendants, or separating God's revelation to Israel from God's revelation in Jesus Christ. To move in either of these directions is to be moving away from orthodox doctrine as the Church of England has received it. The rejection of Marcionism in the second century, noted above, was an affirmation of the unity of God's action through biblical history and of the faithfulness of God's word to Israel, as well as the ordering of that word to the mystery of Christ, affirmed in Article VII. It might be noted that Harnack, mentioned above as one of the figures from modern liberal theology who could be associated with the first response, argued in his study of Marcion that the Old Testament should no longer be regarded as canonical in contemporary Christianity.[57] As with the fourth response, there are potential questions here too about how the Old Testament is to be regarded as Christian Scripture.

The concept of fulfilment – itself multi-layered – has been pivotal for how Christians from the New Testament onwards have sought to affirm that unity. At the centre of the claims Christians make about fulfilment is the death and resurrection of Christ, which happened, in perhaps the oldest formulation of the Christian gospel, 'according to the Scriptures' (1 Corinthians 15.3-4). The new thing God does by raising the crucified

Christ – so radiantly, radically new that it cannot be fully fathomed or grasped – is utterly in accordance with all that God has said and done before. Yet it also changes the way that all that God has said and done before is received, which means that belief and practice cannot simply carry on unaltered. Nonetheless, transformed perception in the light of the good news of Christ of what has been said and done by God in the past cannot lead to the conclusion that it has now been emptied of value, or replaced by something else of the same kind: instead, what has been fulfilled finds its fullness in the new thing God has done, which means its value is newly affirmed and it both deserves and demands our continuing attention as the word and work of God. The letter to the Hebrews gives particularly sustained and close attention to issues arising from that fundamental insight.

For many scholars, Hebrews is a mysterious and difficult text that has been long neglected. This book has re-emerged in biblical study, however, both because of the relationship between Jewish tradition and Christian belief it portrays and because of its use of the Old Testament/Tanakh. For the book of Hebrews, the Old Testament is 'a repository of divine speech' and its words are 'living and active' and, for the author of Hebrews, speak about Jesus, God's Son. The main concern, however, when reading Hebrews is the enduring interpretation from the second century AD onwards that this book promotes the view that Christianity replaces Judaism. Such views are not difficult to hold when reading the comparisons in Hebrews between Jesus' atoning death and the Levitical sacrifices, or the use of the adjective 'better' when comparing priests and covenants.

And yet, Hebrews is written before the definitive 'parting of the ways' described in the previous chapter. With the rich variegation of Judaism in the Second Temple period and processes of self-definition that the destruction of the Temple produced, texts like Hebrews that appear as polemical need not be seen as advocating the first response discussed above or, at an extreme, antisemitism (see especially Hebrews 7.1-12; 8.7-13; and 10.1-10).[58] Both Jews and Christians needed to respond to the destruction of the Temple, whose traumatic effect cannot be over-emphasized. Rabbinic Judaism developed through the 'sacrifice of the heart', in prayer and repentance; Christianity stressed the atoning sacrifice of Jesus 'made once and for all'. Recent arguments have been made to suggest that Hebrews, written after the destruction of the Temple, bears witness to a response to the loss of the Temple and the loss of the Levitical cult. Hebrews never discusses Jewish ritual practice after the Temple's destruction but confines itself to the Levitical system found in Scripture. Thus the caution stands when reading Hebrews not to 'confuse or conflate the religion of Israel – particularly the cultic expression of Israelite religion – with Judaism then (late first/early second century), with Judaism now, or with Judaism in general'.[59]

In what it says that bears directly or indirectly on Christian–Jewish relations, therefore, the Church of England should neither deny the continuing participation of Jewish people in Israel as God's gift and God's creation, nor limit the grace proclaimed in the gospel of Christ, which is 'the power of God for salvation to everyone who has faith, to the Jew first and also to the Greek'. Given these parameters, there is a clear case for preferring approaches that fall within the range of the second and third responses as outlined above. The space between the second and third responses might be marked by how the concluding exclamation at the end of Romans 11 is seen in relation to what comes before:

> 'O the depth of the riches and wisdom and knowledge of God! How
> unsearchable are his judgements and how inscrutable his ways!
> 'For who has known the mind of the Lord? Or who has been his
> counsellor?' 'Or who has given a gift to him, to receive a gift in
> return?' For from him and through him and to him are all things.
> To him be the glory forever. Amen.'

For those advocating the second response, this is likely to be read as a
transposition into the register of praise of the argument Paul has been
carefully setting out in Romans 9–11 as a whole. For those drawn to the
third response, however, it may be regarded as an acknowledgement of
the limit of that argument: that what God has done, is doing and will do
in Israel is an utterly glorious mystery that our best theological thinking
cannot ultimately fathom – that there is a mystery here exceeding our
comprehension.

For both the first and the fourth responses as set out above, the
question of the relationship of Jewish people to Christ is a more or
less closed one: for the first, there can be none (other than that which
pertains to humanity generally) and for the fourth, there is no need for
one. Both the second and third responses, however, can leave open a
certain amount of space at this point. To believe that fulfilment lies for
all in relation to Christ does not mean that it must lie for others in joining
what we perceive to be our present relation to Christ, nor that our
relation may not itself require profound transformation, whose end
will utterly astonish us. It has long been recognized that the phrase
pistis Christou in Paul's letters can be rendered as either 'the faith
[or faithfulness] of Christ' or '[our] faith in Christ'. While the latter
interpretation has been normative in much of the Christian theological

tradition, the former has increasingly been advocated in recent Pauline studies. It places the weight squarely on what Christ has done for us rather than on what we do in relation to him. Is it then possible that some may share in the 'faith of Christ' who do not confess to 'faith in Christ', above all those who call in faith on the God of Israel, to whom 'In the days of his flesh, Jesus offered up prayers and supplications ... and he was heard because of his reverent submission' (Hebrews 5.7)? The unity of the Christian canon of Scripture rests on the identity of the Word who became flesh in Jesus Christ with the Word of God revealed to Israel according to the Old Testament. What may be the continuing relationship to this one divine Word of Jewish people today? While the second and third responses give different parameters for answering that question, both provide scope to ponder it.

A Christian theology of Jewish–Christian relations will inevitably reflect the divergence that, together with kinship, was said to characterize relations between Christianity and Judaism. It will not be something with which Jewish people could be expected simply to agree, while attempts to articulate the disagreement need to be constantly mindful of the way that words such as faith, grace, covenant and salvation are heard by Christian and Jewish people in overlapping but also contrasting ways, as explained in the preceding section. While appreciating these challenges, it will also want to learn from and with Jewish dialogue partners and be always alert to the danger of encouraging inattentive stereotyping that can feed into antisemitism.

A 'sacrament of otherness'?

Within the wide arena of interfaith relations, should Anglicans treat Christian–Jewish relations as a special case?[60] In the contemporary teaching of the Roman Catholic Church, it is recognized both that Christian–Jewish relations require a distinctive theological account, and also that they are not thereby wholly divorced from relations with all other faiths. The parameters for the Church of England's theology of Christian–Jewish relations as set out in the previous section would fit with this position.

The theological distinctiveness is expounded in the Second Vatican Council's 1965 declaration *Nostra Aetate*, which in addressing Christian–Jewish relations affirmed that it was 'sounding the depths of the mystery which is the Church'.[61] On the other hand, the text of *Nostra Aetate* moved from an initial draft focused entirely on the topic *De Judaeis* to become a statement speaking also about relations with Muslims, and more widely with Hindus, Buddhists and other religions. This expansion of the text may have been influenced by political factors, but underpinning it is a theology which sees the distinctiveness of Christian–Jewish relations as being in some sense paradigmatic for all other interfaith relations.[62] The Church's primary and oldest relationship with a religious 'other' is with Judaism. If Christians can learn how to understand and practise that relationship rightly, this may in turn help them in relating to other religions, even if the theological bases of those relationships are different. Reflecting on the significance of *Nostra Aetate*, Cardinal Walter Kasper expressed this in an evocative phrase to which we return below: 'Judaism is as a sacrament of every otherness that as such the Church must learn to discern, recognise and celebrate.'[63]

In so far as an authoritative shape of Anglican theological teaching can be recognized and articulated in this area, it too reflects this sense of a paradigmatic distinctiveness to Christian–Jewish relations. *Jews, Christians and Muslims* asserts: 'A right understanding of the relationship with Judaism is fundamental to Christianity's own self-understanding', and adds that we must 'reject any view of Judaism which sees it as a living fossil, simply superseded by Christianity'.[64] The combination of that affirmation and rejection could be described as 'deutero-Augustinian',[65] in that like St Augustine of Hippo it sees theological significance in the continued existence of Jewish life in the world after Christ. For Augustine, the immediate question was that of the continued toleration of the Jewish people in an Empire that had become legally Christian.[66] Augustine argued that the Roman authorities should safeguard the continuance of Jewish life, by contrast with pagans or heretics. He described the Jews of his time as *librarii nostri* ('our scribes')[67] and *custodes librorum nostrorum* ('guardians of our books'),[68] stewards of the revelation of the God of Israel.

However, that Christians should in this way see theological significance in Jewish people *post Christum* does not in itself imply a 'right understanding of the relationship with Judaism', as the always contested history of Christian–Jewish interaction shows.[69] Augustine's own view was that contemporary Jewish misery was an encouraging proof to Christians of the truth of the gospel since it was a divine punishment for their rejection of the Messiah. Seven centuries later, and in very different circumstances, St Bernard of Clairvaux argued strongly that Jews should not be killed, on the grounds that 'they are living tokens to us, constantly recalling our Lord's passion'.[70] It is easy to see how this Christian *adversus Judaeos* tradition, while on the one hand it preserved a Jewish presence in Christian Europe, also on the other hand contributed to the 'teaching of contempt' identified by Jules Isaac (see page 15 above). This ancient teaching of disparagement in turn shaped the conditions, and provided much of the imagery, which made possible the rise of modern European antisemitism, albeit the latter denied the principle of preservation of Jewish people, which was part of the older Christian anti-Judaism.

Following the lead of the Second Vatican Council,[71] Anglican documents have, as already noted, categorically rejected the teaching of contempt and the antisemitism associated with it, in 1988 in *The Way of Dialogue* and again in 2008 in *Generous Love*.[72] If such a negative account is rightly judged to be unacceptable, requiring a clear break with much of Augustine's legacy in this matter, how might his fundamental commitment to seeing theological significance in Judaism *post Christum* find expression today and thereby contribute to filling out the parameters for the Church of England's understanding, as described in the previous section?[73]

In Romans 9–11, discussed in the previous section, Paul is wrestling at every level, from autobiography through the life of the nascent Christian community, up to the divine purpose for Israel, with the challenge of reconciling his own identity before God. Paul clearly identifies as a Jew in the present tense throughout his letters (Philippians 3; 2 Corinthians 11; Romans 11) and yet he also identifies as one who has been 'crucified with Christ' and who is an apostle with faith in Christ's saving power. Such identities are at the heart of Paul's struggle as throughout his letters and especially in Romans he tries to reconcile them. Ultimately, he cannot do so other than by falling into wonder, love and praise:

'O the depth of the riches and wisdom and knowledge of God! How unsearchable are his judgements and how inscrutable his ways!' (Romans 11.33).

The letter to the Ephesians identifies the reconciliation between Israel and the nations through the cross as lying at the heart of the good news (Ephesians 2.11-22). 'The mystery of Christ' is that 'the Gentiles have become fellow-heirs, members of the same body, and sharers in the promise in Christ Jesus through the gospel' (Ephesians 3.3, 6). The Church is born from this union in which neither Jew nor Gentile can claim to be the norm for the other. Its generative pluriformity through history rests on rendering peaceable the irreducible 'otherness' of Israel and the nations in the one body of Christ (Ephesians 2.14-16). The vision of Ephesians fades quickly in the following centuries, as the Gentile-majority Church discourages or even seeks to ban any expression through Torah observance of the 'otherness' of Israel within its life. That is not to say, however, that the vision disappears altogether.

It is worth at this point recalling Cardinal Kasper's description of Judaism as a 'sacrament of every otherness'. Not all Anglicans will find this language congenial (nor, indeed, all Roman Catholics), but the point being made is that a sacrament is a divinely established sign that reliably conveys to Christian believers the grace and life of God. To speak of Jewish people in the language of 'sacrament' is thus to say that encounter with them can be for Christians a source of blessing, a way of being called back to holiness, a point of connection with the promises of God. Indeed, as a sacrament has about it the further character of reliability based on God's pledge, such encounter is an assured sign of grace set within a relationship of divine promise and human response: it is theologically located within the covenant God has made with his people. While we must be open to the possibility of God's grace operating in many forms of life outside the Christian Church, including many religions, to speak of a 'sacrament of otherness' is to say more than this. It is to say that encounter with the contemporary reality of the faithfulness of Jewish people – in readiness to learn by attentive listening and to be surprised by what is received – can be confidently relied on to be a means of God's grace to us and an occasion for the renewal of our own faith, as we experience in such meeting the intertwining of both our kinship and our divergence.

It is not, therefore, a matter of simply overcoming or setting aside the divergence for a moment of undiluted kinship. What makes this possible is the very difference of Judaism from Christianity. Jewish people, by the continuity and vitality of their existence, defy all attempts to reduce them to mere bearers of Christian meaning, to accommodate them comfortably within a Christian universe of discourse; yet neither can they be left outside it – the 'family' relationship remains. It is precisely through this irreducibility that they can be salutary to us as Christians, when we too readily seek to explain difference in terms familiar to ourselves.[74] Moreover, there is a wider application for Christians in interfaith relations of this 'return of the Jewish other', since it is in remembering and revisiting this first and unique encounter with irreducible difference within a relationship of God-given kinship that the Church can learn the virtues of humility and wonder that prepare it to engage with other expressions of the human before God it cannot make its own. Any serious engagement with any religious other drives us to revisit the first covenant, as the Jewish other shapes our Christian identity in relation to God.

Theology and practice: representing the Christian–Jewish relationship

In Christian art of the Middle Ages, the Church (*ecclesia*) and the Synagogue (*synagoga*) were personified as two women, of contrasting fortunes. The Church is shown erect and triumphant, bearing a cross; the Synagogue is usually blindfolded and dejected, bearing a broken staff and sometimes decorated with the Tablets of the Ten Commandments symbolizing the Old Testament.

In England, the clearest example of such imagery is to be found on the Chapter House door of Rochester Cathedral (you can find a photograph at www.architecture.com/imagelibrary/ribapix/image-information/poster/rochester-cathedral-kent-the-decorated-door-to-the-chapter-house/posterid/RIBA58974.html). While we see many of the typical features, here the two figures, rather than being free-standing, are joined by the arch over the door frame, for which they serve as the base on each side, both supporting the figures it contains.

A contemporary reimagining of this medieval motif can be found outside the Institute for Catholic-Jewish Relations at St Joseph's University in the United States, where there is a statue titled *Synagoga and Ecclesia in Our Time*, reproduced on the cover of this book. It represents a very different relationship between the two female personifications than the one generally portrayed in medieval art.

To what extent does the sculpture from St Joseph's reflect what the relationship between Christianity and Judaism has been like?

How well does it express Christian hopes for what that relationship might become today?

PART 2

Critical Issues

3. **Mission and Evangelism**

Affirmations

The distinctive relationship of kinship and divergence between Christianity and Judaism should cause Christians to think carefully about mission and evangelism in the case of their Jewish neighbours. The Church participates in the mission of God by: 1. Proclaiming the good news of the kingdom; 2. Teaching, baptizing and nurturing new believers; 3. Responding to human need in loving service 4. Seeking to challenge unjust structures in society and 5. Striving to safeguard the integrity of creation. Called to bear witness to the saving love of God in Jesus Christ for all people, Jews as well as Gentiles, the Church remembers with gratitude that Jewish people stand in a unique relationship to the God of Israel who has drawn near to us in Christ. There is a particular responsibility to be attentive to the ways in which evangelism (associated with the first two of the 'marks' of mission as listed above) can be seen as threatening to Jews and ignorant of that unique relationship to God. Conscious of the participation of Christians over the centuries in stereotyping, persecution and violence directed against Jewish people, and how this contributed to the Holocaust, Christians today should be sensitive to Jewish fears. It is important that Christians are mindful that witness to God's grace involves helping to create the conditions for dialogue marked by respect and trust, and that they worship with Jewish people the one God revealed to the patriarchs and prophets and attested to in shared Scriptures, affirmed in the common use of the psalms through the centuries.

The term 'mission' has been explored in great depth in Christian theology in recent decades. It has acquired a rich range of meaning rooted in the sending by the Father of the divine Son and Spirit for the salvation of the world. Anglicans have become familiar with the 'Five Marks of Mission' as one way to encapsulate how the Church participates in the mission of God, as set out in the 'Affirmations' above.[75]

The breadth of this understanding of mission provides scope for considering ways in which Christians may share in God's mission with those outside the Church, including other faiths. In section 3 of its treatment of the 'Way of Sharing', the Anglican Communion document *Jews, Christians and Muslims: The Way of Dialogue* stated: 'Jews, Muslims and Christians have a common mission. They share a mission to the world that God's name may be honoured: "Hallowed be your name."'[76] As well as the hallowing or sanctification of God's name, the Christian imperative to seek the kingdom of God is one that can have especial resonance for Jews, as the Jewish concept of *tikkun olam* ('mending the world') may have for Christians. The potential for fruitful interchange between Jews and Christians on the concept of mission has been explored in a publication that emerged from the Lambeth-Jewish Forum for Christian–Jewish dialogue.[77] With regard to the third, fourth and fifth 'Marks of Mission', there is a degree of overlap with the significant potential for common ground between Christianity and Judaism in ethical understanding and moral action, addressed in the final chapter below.

This chapter focuses instead on some of the difficult questions that occur in this area with regard to the first two 'Marks of Mission', which are linked directly to Christian practices of evangelism that seek to share the gospel of Christ with those who have not received it and to assist them in becoming his disciples. Is it right that Christians engage in evangelism as thus understood with Jewish people who have not embraced the Christian faith? This is a question to which many Christians would think the answer is obvious – for some, obviously yes, and for some, obviously no. If it can be a controversial subject in Christian circles, it is also a highly sensitive one for Christian–Jewish relations, as will be explained more fully below. While there are a range of different factors to be considered, the aim of this chapter is to set out some theological parameters, based on the framework established in Part I of the report.

It may be useful to begin by reviewing the four Christian responses outlined in Chapter 2 to Jewish claims to belong to God's chosen people Israel since the time of Christ, in terms of their implications for this question. For the first response, the unqualified denial of that claim, there would be no reason to regard Jewish people any differently from anyone else who is outside the Church when it comes to seeking their conversion. The answer is therefore the same for them as for anyone else in this category. For the fourth response, the unqualified affirmation of that same claim, conversion to Christian faith that brings Jewish people into the Church is if anything to be actively avoided, as God's purpose for the Jewish people is to remain separate from – if perhaps still in some way related to – the life of the Church. Moreover, there is simply no need for Jewish people to enter into a relationship with Christ, so any kind of witness to the gospel has no point. As it was concluded that both these responses are in various ways inadequate in the light of Christian doctrine, it may be expected that the conclusions that follow from them regarding witness and evangelism are also flawed.

The second and third responses were regarded as encompassing a range of positions, between which there would be significant debate and indeed disagreement, but that are broadly consonant with the Church of England's understanding of doctrine. For both positions, the universality of the gospel as good news for all is affirmed. The Son of God became incarnate to bring fullness of life for all, and the Church is called to witness to that. The primary aim of such witness is not to replicate our relationship to God in others, but to point them faithfully to Christ. The role of the witness is simply to be faithful in that pointing away from self to the one who has spoken and acted. Such witness to Christ need not involve words, but neither will it be afraid to give an account of itself when invited to do so. How others respond to the witness's testimony is not the concern of the witness as such, though because this is believed to be the truth that sets people free, there will be a desire for others to see that truth and know that freedom, without being able to predict what that might mean in every case.

That Christians should bear witness to Christ in this sense in their relations with Jewish people is therefore to be expected. Where there is opportunity for dialogue about matters of faith in this context, the parameters set out in Chapter 2 mean that Christians will want to remember with gratitude that Jewish people stand in a unique relationship to the God of Israel who has drawn near to us in Christ. Where there is an opening for witness to include words, it will therefore be in the context of a dialogue in which Christians expect to learn and receive from Jewish participants. Jewish people have also been called to bear witness to God; Christians will be concerned to attend to that witness also whenever there is an occasion humbly to offer their own. They may expect such encounter in faith between Christians and Jews to be 'sacramental' for them in a certain sense, as was explored in Chapter 2.

The second response to Jewish claims to belong to God's chosen people Israel since the time of Christ was described as 'acceptance qualified with some correction', and the third as 'acknowledgement of mystery'. For many who would locate themselves broadly within the third response, such witness in mutual dialogue would not have as its hoped-for horizon the possibility of Jewish participants converting to Christian faith. Its aim might be articulated instead as growth for all participants in faith, hope and love, through entering more deeply together into the mystery of God's revelation than would be possible in separation from one another. While it would be possible for some Jewish people to be thereby drawn towards Christ as the one in whom faith, hope and love are finally found, such an outcome does not form part of the purpose of witness in dialogue. For those identifying with the second response, on the other hand, there is likely to be a stronger sense both of responsibility to enable Jewish people to hear the message of Jesus Christ as truly good news, and of confidence that the fruit of such encounter God longs to see is the recognition here and now of Jesus Christ as Son of God and Saviour.

Within the range of approaches to Christian–Jewish relations represented by the positions identified in Chapter 2 as most consonant with the Church of England's teaching, some differences of perspective on the place of evangelism are therefore to be expected. This is in some contrast with views that would appear wholly to exclude action motivated by the hope that Jewish people may come to know Christ.[78] Nonetheless, as emphasized above, across this range all should appreciate opportunities to speak with Jewish people about matters of faith as occasions for Christians to listen, receive and learn from the witness of others, while also bearing witness themselves to God's grace 'in a humble and sensitive manner'.[79] The importance of dialogue as the proper context for Christian–Jewish relations was specifically highlighted in the arrangement of Resolution 37 of the 1978 Lambeth Conference, which states:

1. Within the Church's trust of the Gospel, we recognize and welcome the obligation to open exchange of thought and experience with people of other faiths. Sensitivity to the work of the Holy Spirit among them means a positive response to their meaning as inwardly lived and understood. It means also a quality of life on our part which expresses the truth and love of God as we have known them in Christ, Lord and Saviour.

2. We realize the lively vocation to theological interpretation, community involvement, social responsibility, and evangelization which is carried by the Church in areas where Hinduism, Buddhism, Taoism, Confucianism, and Islam are dominant, and ask that the whole Anglican Communion support them by understanding, by prayer, and where appropriate, by partnership with them.

3. We continue to seek opportunities for dialogue with Judaism.[80]

The relevance of the 'Difficult History' outlined in Chapter 1 needs to be especially kept in mind by Christians in reflecting on these matters, as well as the 'Distinctive Relationship' set out in Chapter 2. In the context of widespread antisemitism that saw Jews as inferior or dangerous because of their biological descent, and therefore an undesirable presence within the Church, churches could see support for efforts to bring Jews to Christian faith as an affirmation of their full humanity and of the Church's welcome towards them. So, for instance, the 1897 Lambeth Conference of bishops from the Anglican Communion resolved 'that a more prominent position be assigned to the evangelisation of the Jews in the intercessions and almsgiving of the Church'.[81] In the immediate aftermath of the Holocaust, the World Council of Churches in 1948 commended a report by its Committee on the Christian Approach to the Jews, whose emphatic rejection of antisemitism was noted earlier (page 17 above). Its recognition that 'No people in (God's) one world has suffered more bitterly from the disorder of man than the Jewish people', was set in the context of the strong recommendation that the churches 'recover the universality of our Lord's commission by including the Jewish people in their evangelistic work'.[82] In 1964, the Lutheran World Federation maintained that 'The witness to the Jewish people is inherent in the gospel and in the commission received from Christ'.[83]

While those making such statements may have been motivated in part by the desire to oppose antisemitism within the Church, the history of coercive attempts by Christian authorities to force Jewish people into conversion means that their words were always likely to be heard very differently in the Jewish community. Even when violent coercion ended, legal discrimination against Jewish people who would not adopt Christianity remained a reality in many European societies well into the twentieth century and was in some cases widely supported within the churches. Moreover, reflection on the Holocaust should remind Christians of how the long tradition of rhetoric attacking Jewish 'faithlessness' and 'stubbornness' for not accepting Jesus as Messiah, Lord and Son of God provided a seedbed for the horrors of modern antisemitism. Those who, with the bishops of the 1897 Lambeth Conference, want to support 'the evangelisation of the Jews' need to understand that Jewish people find such language profoundly threatening, with overtones of what has been called 'theological genocide'. In a country such as this one where they form a small minority, the Jewish community can feel vulnerable when faced with the cultural and political influence of the churches, and deeply uncomfortable with the idea that this influence might be deliberately directed at changing the religious adherence of its members.

Some Christians would conclude from this that it is not appropriate for Christians today to seek the conversion of Jewish people to Christianity, because we find ourselves at a point where such activity is inevitably shadowed by a legacy that is bound to trigger mistrust and estrangement. All Christians should perhaps agree that part of the witness that the Church needs to offer in these circumstances is to show repentance for the sins of the past, as called for in the Introduction, and awareness of the long shadow those sins cast into the present. Only on this basis can they begin to build confidence in mutual dialogue where the witness of Christians and Jews to the one God can be truly shared with one another.

In Christian teaching, God's covenant and election are always ordered towards Jesus Christ, the Son of God who became incarnate for the salvation of the world and who offers fullness of life to all, including Jewish people.[84] The person of Jesus Christ cannot therefore but be a continuing subject for Christian–Jewish dialogue where the Church witnesses to a belief in the incarnation, with Jesus being 'the image of the invisible God' (Colossians 1.15) revealed in the Old Testament.

Christians engaging in such dialogue should not be afraid to speak of the glory they see in Christ, while also being attentive to the different perspectives Jewish readers will bring to passages of shared Scripture Christians may relate to God's work in him.[85]

In Christian history, alongside the shameful accounts of forced conversions to Christianity and conversions from Judaism as practical accommodations to religious and cultural disadvantage and avoidance of discrimination, there are also stories of free and genuine conversions by Jews to the way of Jesus Christ, as there are stories of Christians converting to Judaism. The border between the two religions has never been entirely closed.[86] Such conversion can also bring significant challenges. As noted in Chapter 1, Jewish converts to Christianity were sometimes regarded with distrust by the Church, as well as with hostility from the Jewish community, while they could also be celebrated and made a focus for public attention. From the nineteenth century onwards, some have suggested that 'Hebrew Christians' need a form of separate and special provision, for instance worshipping in the Hebrew language, rather than being integrated into Gentile congregations. The emergence over the last fifty years of the movement known as 'Messianic Judaism' raises some difficult questions for the historic churches while also being viewed with considerable suspicion by other Jews, so that those identifying with it may find themselves feeling doubly marginalized. The issues raised by conversions between Christianity and Judaism as a religious phenomenon are complex; addressing them does not fall within the scope of this chapter, which has focused on the implications of Christian theology of Christian–Jewish relations for witness and evangelism on the part of the Church.[87]

Theology and practice: mission to or ministry among?

The Church of England has its own history of evangelism specifically addressed to Jewish people. The London Society for promoting Christianity among the Jews (LSCJ) was founded in 1809 with the support of prominent Anglican Evangelicals as a missionary society for the conversion of Jewish people, as well as educating the Church about its Jewish roots, and it has numbered notable Anglican supporters over the years. At its peak in 1914 it had around 280 mission staff, with around a third of those being of Jewish descent.

LSCJ has undergone changes in name since its establishment in the nineteenth century that point to the changing context for its continuing work. It became CMJ, Church Missions to Jews, then The Church's Mission to the Jews, next The Church's Ministry Among the Jews, and finally, today, The Church's Ministry Among Jewish People. These shifts in name reveal something of the questions around the nature of the Christian relationship with Jewish people where a task of ministry, being with, and among, seems to be a more appropriate approach than a mission to. Changing attitudes are also reflected in the decision taken in 1992 by the new Archbishop of Canterbury, Dr George Carey, to end 150 years of tradition and decline to become the patron of the charity. For an overview of CMJ today, see the website at www.cmj.org.uk/about/.

In what ways is the gospel of Jesus Christ good news for Jewish people?

Should it be shared, and if so, in what contexts?

4. Teaching and Preaching

Affirmations

In teaching, preaching, liturgy and more informal modes of communication within their communities, Christians, clergy and lay, should provide a truthful and accurate representation of biblical and Rabbinic Judaism and of Jesus as a Jew of his time who came not to destroy the Law and the Prophets but to fulfil them. This requires awareness of the substantial theological and scriptural continuities between Judaism and Christianity as well as understanding of the new thing that God has done in Christ. Sensitivity is needed to implicit or explicit references to Jews or Judaism in liturgy and in the public reading of Scripture, in hymnody and in artistic representations, which can be misunderstood or can reinforce prejudices. When Christians seek to draw positively on Jewish liturgy and traditions for Christian worship, they should do so with awareness that Judaism is a living and developing religion with its own integrity.

As the churches have sought to repudiate theological perspectives that have given legitimation to antisemitism, including the 'teaching of contempt', and to affirm the continuing place of the Jewish people within the purposes of God, questions about how to teach and preach the faith have come under careful scrutiny. To what extent does teaching and practice that passes on Christian faith – from sermons and church-based education to hymnody and iconography – also pass on, however inadvertently, an anti-Judaism that is used to provide a rationale for antisemitism? Where texts or objects can be understood in ways that are no longer acceptable, should they be rendered inconspicuous or removed altogether, can they be altered and adapted, or is the solution to provide a clear commentary on both their past history and their contemporary interpretation?

The Roman Catholic Church has taken a lead in addressing these issues. Building on the ground-breaking principles of *Nostra Aetate* (1965), the Vatican Commission for Religious Relations with Jews issued guidance for preaching and catechesis in 1985 that emphasized the need to educate against antisemitism.[88] The World Council of Churches has also published a series of relevant documents, including 'Ecumenical Considerations on Jewish–Christian Dialogue' (1982). Section 3.2 notes:

> Teachings of contempt for Jews and Judaism in certain Christian traditions proved a spawning ground for the evil of the Nazi Holocaust. The Church must learn so to preach and teach the Gospel as to make sure that it cannot be used towards contempt for Judaism and against the Jewish people.[89]

In an Anglican context, *Jews, Christians and Muslims*, from the 1988 Lambeth Conference, emphasized the need for continued examination of teaching and preaching. The Church of England's discussion document *Sharing One Hope?* also highlighted the importance of liturgy and ministerial training in this respect.[90] *Common Worship: Times and Seasons*, in its introduction to the season of Passiontide and Holy Week, includes a paragraph on the historic role of this season in encouraging hostility to Jews.[91] It emphasizes the importance of being 'sensitive to the ways in which an unreflecting use of traditional texts (like the Reproaches) can perpetuate a strain of Christian anti-Semitism'. The collect for Good Friday in the Book of Common Prayer referring to 'all Jews, Turks, Infidels and Hereticks' does not appear in revised liturgies.

Truthful and accurate representation of Jews and Judaism in Christian teaching helps to disentangle the teaching of the gospel from the legacy of anti-Judaism and antisemitism, and to foster respect and love for the Jewish people through whom God acted in Jesus. Such rigour and accuracy will avoid any lingering presence of the 'teaching of contempt' that has sometimes characterized the perspective on Jews within Christian worship.[92] Lay and ordained teachers and preachers, including those who work with children and young people, have a particular responsibility to correct untrue negative images of Judaism in their interpretation and exposition of biblical texts.

There are undoubtedly difficult passages for Christian–Jewish relations in the New Testament, whose interpretation has been used to perpetuate both antisemitism and anti-Judaism (see pages 12-16 above). 'Pharisees' continue to be invoked in Christian teaching and preaching as characterized by a devotion to the detail of human religious tradition at odds with true reverence for the word of God and love of one's human neighbour. Not only is this a caricature that would be questioned by contemporary historical scholarship, it is also deeply hurtful to many Jews who number the Pharisaic teachers among those who maintained the tradition of Torah by which they live today.

Traditional interpretations of parables such as the Pharisee and the Tax Collector or the Labourers in the Vineyard can contribute to the stereotyping of Jews as those who adhere to a false and sinful perversion of true faith in God. Ironically, even the parable of the Good Samaritan, with its roots in Deuteronomy, illustrating neighbourly duty within a context of contempt and conflict, can be presented in such a way as to foster contempt for others who care about certain forms of religious observance different from our own. Much work has been done on demonstrating how one might read many of the parables as the first (Jewish) hearers would have understood them, although questions remain about the relationship between such understanding and the interpretation of the Evangelists themselves.[93] Preaching, teaching and scripture study are not neutral activities and it is incumbent upon those so engaged to ensure that they are not handing on misleading stereotypes found in material produced by others, including material that has much of continuing value in other respects.

The presentation of 'the Jews' at certain points in John's Gospel as opposed to Jesus has also been used to impute a collective involvement for the Jewish people in confounding the purposes of God. It has been suggested that the translation of *hoi Ioudaioi* in this context as 'the Jews' rather than 'the Judaeans', for example, when it could conceivably mean either, ignores the contemporary tensions between Galileans and Judaeans and runs counter to the evident acceptance by the Gospel writer that Jesus and his followers were also 'Jews'.[94] Not all have been convinced by this argument, and other scholars have debated whether it is the 'religious' or the 'ethnic' aspect of the term that should be stressed in this context; like 'the Jews' in English, *hoi Ioudaioi* in Greek encompasses both, leading others to argue that both aspects are relevant in the Fourth Gospel.[95]

Such concerns become especially acute in the case of a passage such as John 8, where Jesus challenges his hearers' references to Abraham, saying: 'You are from your father the devil' (John 8.44). Scholars have written extensively on both the literary construction of the passage to juxtapose a theme of light and darkness, and on how it may reflect conflicts between the Johannine community, the wider Church and Jewish leaders.[96] The harshness of the language must also be seen in the context of the rhetoric of the day and, albeit in a different context, in the tradition of prophetic warnings. Nonetheless, varying theological emphases within the Church of England regarding the doctrine of scriptural inspiration and authority may have a bearing on how such concerns are addressed: must a way of reading such 'difficult texts' be found that enables them to be understood as reflecting divinely revealed truth about the Jewish people, or can it be accepted that words attributed to Christ by the Gospel writers may remain marked by human conflicts and limitations?

The condemnation of Jews throughout the centuries as 'Christ killers', integral to the 'teaching of contempt' identified by Jules Isaac, could try to appeal for justification to Matthew 27.25: 'Then the people as a whole answered, "His blood be upon us and on our children!"' This and other texts from the Passion of Christ in the Gospels therefore need to be given particular care in Christian teaching and worship today.[97] Christian theological focus is on the willing sacrifice of Jesus: it is the blood of Jesus that delivers from sin and from divine judgement, covering all transgressions. Moreover, to receive the benefits of Christ's Passion, we must recognize ourselves as those who have contributed to it: if we do not primarily see ourselves in all those who oppose and reject him in the Gospels and prefer to find in them those to whom we count ourselves superior, we separate ourselves from his grace. As the then Archbishop of Canterbury, Michael Ramsey, said in a public statement from 1964:

Those who crucified Christ are in the true mind of the Christian Church representatives of the whole human race, and it is for no one to point a finger of resentment at those who brought Jesus to his death, but rather to see the crucifixion as the divine judgement upon all humanity for choosing the way of sin rather than the Love of God. We must all see ourselves judged by the crucifixion of Christ'.[98]

It is noteworthy that such an approach is reflected in the way that the resources for Good Friday in *Common Worship* adapt and interpret some of the traditional texts.

New Testament texts that represent conflict between Jesus and other Jewish teachers and between the early Christian movement and the Judaism within which it originated present some of the most direct challenges for those who teach and preach in the Church. The challenges are there whether the context is an act of worship, educational work (with adults or with children and young people, where unhelpful simplification may be a particular temptation), or an informal Bible study in someone's home. Addressing these texts in any context presents opportunities to receive the gospel and grow in discipleship – but always with the risk of repeating negative stereotypes of Jewish people, and thereby perhaps unintentionally obstructing positive engagement with Judaism as a living reality and perpetuating the conditions that help the virus of antisemitism to survive.

There are also significant opportunities and challenges in the way that Christians teach and preach from the Old Testament. One of the features that can be found across a range of different traditions in the contemporary Church of England is the decline in frequency of reading from and preaching on Old Testament texts week by week in Sunday services. At the same time, the expectations set down in the Book of Common Prayer of daily sharing by the Christian community in praying and praising with the psalms, including on Sundays, find only a weak response in much contemporary church practice. As was emphasized in Chapter 2, one of the foundations for Christian–Jewish relations is the overlapping of our scriptural canons, underlined, for Christians, by the fact that Tanakh as it existed in first-century Palestine was the only Bible that our Lord Jesus Christ knew, the Scripture from which he taught and preached. It is therefore vital for Christian–Jewish relations today that the Old Testament in all its wonderful breadth and rich diversity is known and treasured by the Church, not least in its public worship and in its programmes of preaching and teaching.

The importance of dialogue with Judaism has been stressed repeatedly in this document. Christians should be aware that Old Testament texts are also being read and studied by Jewish people who will in some cases interpret them differently from inherited traditions of Christian understanding. Christians can learn much from Jewish tradition, as they can from contemporary Jewish scholarship,[99] aware that in some instances divergence arises from fundamental points of disagreement between Christianity and Judaism. Nonetheless, on specific points of exegesis, some Christians will agree with some Jews and disagree with some other Christians.

Those who teach and preach in the Church of England should avoid implying that the meaning of Old Testament prophecy points to Christ in such a direct and obvious way that anyone who denies it must be refusing to pay attention to the text or be somehow defective in their understanding. Such implications feed directly into the negative stereotyping of Jewish people that forms the fundamental structure of antisemitism (see page 11 above).

At the same time, care needs to be taken to avoid the opposite danger of distancing the Church from Israel in the Old Testament, as if they had no abiding relation to one another. God is named in the New Testament also as the God of Israel. The Church is the body of Christ, who is the anointed one of Israel. Perhaps the earliest summary of the gospel message in the New Testament says 'that Christ died for our sins according to the Scriptures, that he was buried, that he was raised on the third day according to the Scriptures' (1 Corinthians 15.3b-4, NIV): if the promises of God in Israel's Scriptures find their 'yes' in Christ (2 Corinthians 1.19-20), then it is also true that the work of God in Christ can only be understood in the light of those Scriptures. As was stressed in Chapter 2, Christian doctrine teaches the unity of God's revelation, so that as hearers of God's word we stand in a relationship of fellowship and solidarity with those who receive that word in every age, testifying with them that the steadfast love of the one Lord never ceases but endures for ever.

Those who preach and teach and who officiate in public worship therefore need to be attentive to how the relationship between Old and New Testaments and between Israel and the Church is being presented. This might include reflection on how different Eucharistic Prayers narrate the story of God's saving work. The choice of 'related' or 'continuous' Old Testament readings for the Principal Service on Sundays during some periods of ordinary time in the Church of England's lectionary provides a different emphasis in opportunities for teaching in this area. Consideration should be given to the use of the 'continuous' lectionary *because all share in the responsibility for Christ's suffering and death, for all have sinned*

strand in some years at least, as an opportunity to focus on the riches of the Old Testament and to encourage the congregation to receive God's word in their reading and hearing of it.

Together with accurate and truthful handling of Scripture, there needs to be sensitive attention to liturgical prayers and hymns in Christian worship and teaching. An example would be one of the verses of Charles Wesley's well-known hymn, 'Lo, He Comes with Clouds Descending':

> Every eye shall now behold him
> Robed in dreadful majesty;
> Those who set at nought and sold him,
> Pierced and nailed him to the tree,
> Deeply wailing, deeply wailing, deeply wailing,
> Shall the true Messiah see.

It is possible to read lines 3–6 and imagine they are about the Jewish people as collectively guilty of crucifying the Messiah, who when he comes again in power and glory recognize – too late? – the terrible crime they have committed. Understood in that way, they convey the 'teaching of contempt' which the Church of England now rejects. If that were the only way to read them, they should no longer be sung in public worship. Yet it is also possible to read lines 3–6 as an amplification of lines 1–2: the 'eye' of every human being is the eye of 'those who set at nought and sold him', because all share in the responsibility for Christ's suffering and death, for all have sinned, and it is the realization of that responsibility that leads to contrition and recognition of him as 'the true Messiah' in his suffering and death for us who caused his pain. Indeed, the whole verse is clearly based on Revelation 1.7, which states that 'on his account all the tribes of the earth will wail'. As was stressed above on pages 65–6 above, if we fail to locate ourselves as 'Those who set at nought and sold him' and instead look askance at the failings of others while finding ourselves justified, we have no share in the benefits of his Passion. Some will nonetheless consider it advisable to replace 'Those' at the beginning of line 3 with 'We', to make sure the congregation understand the verse in this second way, and not the first. Others might argue that the second way is evidently the right one, and it does not need to be underlined by amendment to the text, though a brief comment from the officiant might help to remove any doubt.[100]

Those officiating at any act of public worship in the Church of England carry a responsibility to ensure that services 'should be reverent and seemly and shall be neither contrary to, nor indicative of any departure from, the doctrine of the Church of England' (Canon B 5.3). Prayers, hymns or juxtapositions of lectionary texts that could encourage the idea that there is something inherently wrong with the Jewish people – suggested at page 11 above as the basic premise of much historic antisemitism – need to be either set aside or accompanied by careful teaching and commentary that acknowledges these dangers and points in a different direction.[101]

Iconography is also significant here. Vestiges of the kind of teaching about Judaism no longer considered acceptable today are evident, for instance, in the figures of triumphant Ecclesia and downcast Synagoga on the west front of Rochester Cathedral presented in the discussion panel at the end of Chapter 2, while the shrines of William of Norwich and Little Hugh of Lincoln, presented in the discussion panel at the end of Chapter 1, provide visible evidence of the origins of the 'blood libel' that served as a catalyst for the mass murder and expulsion of Jewish communities in medieval England. In both these cases, careful thought has been given by the cathedral authorities as to how these features of their buildings should be explained to pilgrims and visitors. The former shrine of William of Norwich has become a place where prayers of repentance are said for all that in our world leads to hatred and violence.

A source of tension between some Jews and Christians is the not uncommon practice of holding a Christian version of the Passover Seder meal, usually during Holy Week. Some Jews are understandably critical of this, as it can be viewed as an appropriation of Jewish liturgy, much as Christians might, for example, be wary of a non-Christian organization adapting Holy Communion liturgy to promote an alternative history of Jesus' last days. Moreover, there is a historical incongruity in Christians seeking to connect themselves with events that took place several decades before the destruction of the Temple by using a rite that reflects the Jewish community's struggle to come to terms with the Temple's loss.[102] This may in turn reinforce unhelpful notions of Judaism today as simply the religion of Jesus' contemporaries, frozen in time ever since. Where a Christian version of the 'Last Supper' is sensitively done, however, those attending report a greater understanding of the Passover and how Jesus and the disciples would have come to view subsequent events, although where a Seder meal leads into a eucharistic service, the clashes of approach become apparent. Sometimes congregations 'adapt' the wording of the Seder to reflect Christian theology, but the merging of liturgy from Christian and non-Christian sources raises questions that need very careful consideration. A less controversial practice is the invitation to a rabbi or Jewish teacher to take a 'demonstration' Seder meal, in which those attending can participate fully.

Theology and practice: how should we pray for the Jewish people on Good Friday?

From an early period, Christians have prayed specifically for the Jewish people on Good Friday. As the Church gave thanks for the salvation of the whole world through the cross of Christ, it was perhaps especially conscious of those who could not join it. Thus prayers for the Jewish people were linked with prayers for others outside the Christian Church.

The Third Collect for Good Friday in the Church of England's Book of Common Prayer reflects that long-standing tradition, and indeed is based on much earlier liturgical texts:

> O Merciful God, who hast made all men, and hatest nothing that thou hast made, nor wouldest the death of a sinner, but rather that he should be converted and live: Have mercy upon all Jews, Turks, Infidels and Hereticks, and take from them all ignorance, hardness of heart, and contempt of thy word: and so fetch them home, blessed Lord, to thy flock, that they may be saved among the remnant of the true Israelites, and be made one fold under one shepherd, Jesus Christ our Lord, who liveth and reigneth with thee and the Holy Spirit, one God, world without end. Amen.

Compare this with the parallel section from the 'Prayers of Intercession' in the service for Good Friday from *Common Worship: Times and Seasons*:

> *Minister* Let us pray for God's ancient people, the Jews, the first to hear his word:
>> for greater understanding between Christian and Jew,
>> for the removal of our blindness and bitterness of heart,

that God will grant us grace to be faithful to his covenant
and to grow in the love of his name.

Silence is kept.

Lord, hear us.

All **Lord, graciously hear us.**

President Lord God of Abraham,
bless the children of your covenant, both Jew and Christian;
take from us all blindness and bitterness of heart,
and hasten the coming of your kingdom,
when the Gentiles shall be gathered in,
all Israel shall be saved,
and we shall dwell together in mutual love and peace
under the one God and Father of our Lord Jesus Christ.

All **Amen.**

The Minister then proceeds to pray in general terms for 'those
who do not believe the gospel of Christ', without naming any
specific groups.

*What theology of Christian–Jewish relations is being conveyed in
the contemporary prayers for Good Friday, and how is it different
from the earlier Collect?*

*If the Church of England's perspective on how to pray for the
Jewish people has changed, does it matter that the sixteenth-
century Collect remains part of its authorized worship?*

5. The Land of Israel

Affirmations

The Holy Land, the land of God's promise, has a significance for Jews and for Christians beyond the significance of all other lands. It has been the source of continuing hope for Jewish people through millennia of exile and dispersion. Many Christians also treasure it as the place where Jesus Christ lived, died and was raised from the dead, where the earliest Christian believers gathered as his witnesses and a continuous Christian presence has been maintained ever since, and where through pilgrimage Christians from every place and nation may find their faith renewed. While Christians will take different approaches to a number of contemporary questions regarding the State of Israel, all should accept that (a) most Jews consider Zionism an important and legitimate aspect of Jewish identity, (b) the State of Israel has a right to a secure existence within recognized and secure borders according to the common principles of international law, (c) the principles of international law also guarantee the rights and security of the Palestinian people, (d) the current apparent impasse presents grave moral difficulties and is ultimately untenable.

In 1948, the Lambeth Conference described the situation in Palestine, and the emergence of the State of Israel as a Jewish 'national homeland',[103] as a 'spiritual question that touches a nerve centre of the world's religious life'. The same sentence including the words 'nerve centre' was also used later that year in the first Assembly of the World

Council of Churches in Amsterdam. Seventy years on, the significance of Israel still seems to touch such a nerve centre. Why? It is a question that Christians cannot – and should not – ignore.

The contemporary relationship between Christians and Jews is inevitably influenced by the reality and significance of the State of Israel. Indeed, questions about how to respond to that reality have become increasingly contested within the Christian churches over the past seventy years, at times generating significant tensions in Christian–Jewish relations. This chapter, after briefly reviewing the development of the State of Israel and its significance for Jewish people, outlines some of the more prominent Christian responses and the theology that underpins them, before providing an evaluation of those responses in the light of the theological perspective developed in Part I.

The State of Israel and the Jewish people

Although international willingness, expressed through the United Nations, to support the establishment of a Jewish state in 1947 was undoubtedly partly a response to the recent unprecedented horrors of the Holocaust, most Jews saw this political development as the only practical solution to the perennial evil of antisemitism and persecution, while many also viewed it as the culmination of their religious hopes over the previous 2000 years.[104]

The liturgy of Passover, the Jewish commemoration of the liberation from Egypt, celebrated each year in Jewish homes, includes the prayer that the participants will be able to eat the Passover meal 'next year in Jerusalem', while the Amidah, the central prayer of the Jewish liturgy, used on a daily basis by religious Jews, in its traditional form beseeches God for return to Jerusalem and to Zion. Parallel passages might be cited from the liturgy for the Day of Atonement and indeed from the words for grace to be said after meals.

There has continued to be a Jewish presence in the land since biblical times, and the phenomenon of some returning to it from the Diaspora for religious reasons stretches back across the centuries. Nevertheless, it was in the second half of the nineteenth century that migration by Jews to the territory then called Palestine began on a significant scale, prompted in part by violent attacks on Jewish communities, especially in Eastern Europe. What became known as Zionism, an organized Jewish movement to facilitate Jewish return to the land of Israel, developed from this.[105] There are many perceptions and definitions of Zionism; more generally, it can be used to refer to the 'historic and continuing desire of the Jewish people for a homeland in the Middle East', and it is this sense that is intended in the rest of this chapter.[106] Many early Zionists were not traditionally religious Jews – some, in fact, were anti-religious secularists – but they still had a deep sense of identification with the 'land', seeing the Bible as a witness to Jewish history and geography. Initially Zionism was opposed by significant Jewish religious leaders, partly because of its secular character, partly because they felt it involved 'forcing the redemption' (only God could bring about the return), partly because they feared it would increase antisemitism, rather than, as Theodor Herzl argued, diminish it. Today, however, the vast majority of Jews support the existence of the State of Israel, although there would be a variety of views on its actions and policies.

The Holocaust and the emergence of the State of Israel have both played a part in encouraging religious reflection on 'Israel' as land and nation. Nonetheless, it should also be remembered that biblical and theological considerations do not play a large part in how a substantial section of Jewish Israelis today view their country.

Although not all Jews today would call themselves Zionist, most would, certainly in the United Kingdom. Part of the context here is that Jews in the UK today are, for the most part, tied spiritually and emotionally to the land of Israel. Many have family living there and a number hold joint Israeli and UK passports. Children at Jewish schools and in synagogue classes in this country learn about Israel in a positive context from an early age. The vast majority of Jews from the UK who visit Israel see the very best of the country: a technologically advanced society with a majority-Jewish identity, schools and institutions. Few visit the Palestinian communities in the West Bank; many are very fearful of doing so, although a range of Jewish organizations offer opportunities for encounter. Not only is Israel the one country in the world whose national holidays reflect the Jewish calendar, where Hebrew is spoken and where kosher food is widely available, but it is also viewed as the 'safe haven' in a world that, given past history, cannot truly be trusted.[107]

It is in the light of the deep and far-reaching relationship between Jewish people and both the land and the State of Israel that the significance needs to be understood of some of the examples of antisemitism given in the IHRA definition cited in Chapter 1 (pages 9–11). These included:

- Denying the Jewish people their right to self-determination, e.g., by claiming that the existence of a State of Israel is a racist endeavor.

- Applying double standards by requiring of it a behavior not expected or demanded of any other democratic nation.

The IHRA definition makes it clear that it is not antisemitic to apply to the State of Israel the same standards of justice that are used with regard to other democratic nations, and, as in the case of other democratic nations, there are bound to be some serious debates about what it is that those standards require in relation to specific issues. The political impetus in the British contexts to protest against perceived injustice by Israel has, however, in many instances disregarded the fear and distress involved for Jewish people here, especially for young Jews at university in the United Kingdom. While fear of being labelled 'antisemitic' should not prevent genuine political discourse, it is the case that some of the approaches and language used by pro-Palestinian advocates are indeed reminiscent of what could be called traditional antisemitism, including its Christian forms, and Christians need to be aware of how this can increase tensions between Jews and Christians in Britain.

Christian theological responses

There is a tradition of Christian support for the return of the Jewish people to their ancient homeland and their establishment there in sovereignty going all the way back to late sixteenth-century England.[108] This view is known as 'Christian Restorationism' as well as 'Christian Zionism'. Its advocates saw it as predicted in prophecy and associated it with the Second Coming of Christ. Christian Restorationism differed from traditional Jewish religious Zionism, which equally looked for a return to the Land, in that it advocated taking practical steps to bring about the return, and, particularly in the nineteenth century, its representatives lobbied the British government hard to use its diplomatic and military power to this end. Traditional religious Zionism rejected practical, political measures as 'forcing the redemption': the restoration should be left to God and his Messiah. Christian Restorationism pre-dated modern political Zionism, and when political Zionism arose within the Jewish community in the late nineteenth century, many Christian restorationists gave it their enthusiastic support. The Balfour Declaration of 1917 affirmed the sympathy of the British government for 'the establishment in Palestine of a national home for the Jewish people ... it being clearly understood that nothing shall be done which may prejudice the civil and religious rights of existing non-Jewish communities in Palestine'. This declaration, which was a first step in a chain of events which led to the Declaration of the State of Israel, was not only prompted by Jewish Zionist aspirations, but was influenced by Christian Restorationism as well.[109]

The term 'Christian Zionism' has subsequently become widely used to describe Christian support for a Jewish homeland or state on explicitly Christian theological grounds.[110] As noted in the Introduction, the Anglican Communion's Network for Inter Faith Concerns produced *Land of Promise?* in 2012, in response to questions about this area. The Anglican Consultative Council passed a resolution in 2012 expressing its appreciation for the report and asking 'that it be made available as a resource for the Provinces to study'.[111]

Land of Promise? looks at the range of views that can be referred to as 'Christian Zionism'. These include approaches that make apocalyptic predictions in which Jews and Judaism are assigned roles in a drama that involves violent conflicts, usually based on a version of 'dispensationalism', a theory popularized in the nineteenth century by J. N. Darby.[112] Such views have become increasingly significant in the last fifty years, especially among Evangelical Christians in the United States, with political implications in Israel and the Western world.

It is inaccurate and unhelpful if Christian theological support for the continuing existence of the State of Israel, whether or not it would describe itself as Christian Zionism, is simply treated as a form of fundamentalism.[113] Some Christian theologians who have a very different perspective from fundamentalism would nonetheless want to explore the resources available within the Christian tradition for positive theological reflection on the contemporary significance of the land and State of Israel. These include, for instance, the recent attempts by the Roman Catholic theologian Gavin D'Costa to outline a 'minimal Catholic Zionism' with very carefully defined limits. A significant theological exploration of Israel as land and state may be found in the lecture prepared for a 2004 conference in Jerusalem by the then Archbishop of Canterbury, Dr Rowan Williams.[114] Not everyone who might be placed on this spectrum would describe their position as Zionist. Some would draw a distinction between support for the right of the State of Israel to a secure existence, for which they would want to make a case on theological grounds, and Zionism as active engagement in defending and developing the State of Israel, for which they would not.

If Christian theology has sometimes been invoked to give support for the State of Israel, it has also been drawn on as a source for resistance to its actions. Some Christians set against the claims of political Zionism the sharp challenge of a Palestinian narrative of dispossession, oppression and discrimination, and on that basis question on moral grounds the

legitimacy of Israel as a Jewish state. A significant development over the
past thirty years has been the development of what is called Palestinian
Christian liberation theology, which has grown out of the experience of
the Palestinian Christian community and its shared concerns with other
Palestinians for upholding human rights.[115] One of the best-known
expressions of such theology is the *Kairos Palestine* document, for which
an ecumenical group of Palestinian Christians were responsible.[116] Since
its publication in 2009 this document has been widely disseminated
among Western Christian groups. It speaks with passion and eloquence
a 'word of faith, hope and love' about the current realities experienced
by the Palestinian people.

The ethical traditions of both Judaism and Christianity are deeply rooted
in and draw from their shared Scripture, both the Torah/Pentateuch
and the prophetic canon, in which the concepts of *mishpat* (justice)
and *tzedaqah* (righteousness) have a powerful voice. The importance
of justice and peace-making in Israel and Palestine is therefore a
valid topic for Christians to discuss, especially with Jewish dialogue
partners.[117] Indeed, the Jewish statement *Dabru Emet*, written by
representatives of different strands of Judaism, specifically affirms
that 'Jewish tradition mandates justice for all non-Jews who reside in
a Jewish state.'[118]

Christians around the world have particular reasons for being concerned
for the well-being of their fellow Christians in Israel and Palestine, as well
as the Middle East more widely, and for feeling a special duty of care for
them. Many treasure the Holy Land as the place where Jesus Christ
lived, died and was raised from the dead, where the earliest Christian
believers gathered as his witnesses and a continuous Christian

presence has been maintained ever since, and where through pilgrimage Christians from every place and nation may find their faith renewed. Many are also aware that for the Palestinian Christian communities who sustain that presence today, the current political and economic realities continue to create substantial hardship and are acting as an incentive to emigrate. Many Palestinians, including Christians, feel that their experience of tragedy and exile in 1948, for which the term Nakba ('Catastrophe') is increasingly used, is often overlooked or deliberately ignored both within Israel and by the international community. At a conference held at Lambeth Palace in July 2011 in support of Christians in Israel and Palestine, the then Archbishop of Canterbury, Rowan Williams, reflected that 'It is a kind of gnosticism ... a kind of cutting loose from history if we say that the presence of our brothers and sisters in the land of Our Lord does not matter to us.'[119]

Evaluation

The theological approach to Christian–Jewish relations advocated in this document can encompass Christian Zionism and Palestinian liberation theology and indeed the dialogue between them – but only within certain limits. The promises of God to Israel, for instance, cannot be separated from what God has done in Christ, and the fulfilment of those promises must correspond with who God has shown himself to be in Jesus Christ, as both servant and Lord of all.

So far as forms of Christian Zionism are concerned that are bound up with apocalyptic speculation, the Church must be clear that there can be no justification in Christian doctrine for setting aside the ordinary requirements of justice for the sake of supposed prophetic fulfilment, when justice is at the heart of God's promises for us. If certain expressions of Christian Zionism would propose that some people within the land of Israel should have no rights – or indeed that others there hold no responsibility for them – then they need to be firmly rejected.

The vision presented to us in Psalm 85 is that 'righteousness and peace will kiss each other' (Psalm 85.10b). Christians and Jews long together for the fullness of righteousness and peace in the places where those words were first sung, including Jerusalem, city of peace (according to one etymology), with its historic and continuing importance to Christianity and Islam as well as to Judaism. The vision of Jerusalem 'as a city open to the adherents of all three religions, where they can meet and live together', is affirmed by many Christians.[120] Although a theological ambivalence about 'holy places' runs deep through much of Christianity, the long tradition of Christian pilgrimage witnesses to the importance Jerusalem has always held for many Christians. Christians are very conscious of the central role the city of Jerusalem, the place to which Jesus deliberately set his face and over which he wept in sorrow, has played in our story of salvation. *Land of Promise?* reflects on the 'sacramental' quality of Jerusalem for Christianity, the way that it acts both as 'a symbol of peace and sign of conflict'.[121]

If the approach taken here raises questions for some aspects of Christian Zionism, the same also applies to certain applications of liberation theology to the Palestinian situation. One of the reasons some have found it difficult to engage positively with the *Kairos Palestine* document is its apparent espousal of something like the first position outlined in Chapter 2, the 'unqualified denial of the claim of Jewish people since the time of Christ to be part of God's chosen people'. It is possible to make a connection here with the way that it seems to call into question the legitimacy of Israel as in any sense a Jewish state.[122] Indeed, views like this have some currency within the Palestinian community, and among supporters of Palestinian rights. These features of the document also create significant difficulties for Christians who might wish to use it as a tool for enabling a discussion on the current political situation with Jewish counterparts.

Related problems occur in considering some of the theological work on this subject produced in Western contexts, such as the rejection of any expression of Zionism as 'exceptionalism'.[123] Christian theology cannot simply eliminate the possibility that God chooses some people and some places for particular roles in the fulfilment of God's purposes.[124] To be chosen by God for a specific purpose, however, is in no sense to be exempted from the commands of love and justice that are addressed to all humanity.

It is certainly true that much of traditional Christianity has viewed the language in the Old Testament about land, and particularly divine promises connected to it, as pointing to, and being fulfilled and universalized through, the ministry of Christ. Inevitably the Jewish reading of the same passages is different. It is telling that, unlike the Christian Old Testament which ends with the book of Malachi and the longing for a Messianic messenger such as Elijah, the Jewish Tanakh concludes with 2 Chronicles and the beginning of the return to Jerusalem from exile in Babylon, an intended prototype in Jewish eyes for return from later exiles. Christians cannot expect to 'read off' from the pages of the Old Testament a script for the unfolding apocalyptic future and the place of the State of Israel within that. Yet neither can they simply dismiss what is said about people and land in the Old Testament as now irrelevant. In Chapter 2, it was argued that for Paul and for us, it matters in the purposes of God that the Jewish people remain as Israel, alongside the Church. The case that this requires some continuing relation of the Jewish people to the land of Israel can be made on theological grounds as well as pragmatic ones, without predetermining the answer to the question of what political arrangements may best secure and express that relation.

Finally, Christians need to be sure that theological consideration of this subject is not influenced by the trope of the 'wandering Jew', which has played a considerable role in Christian history. For example, a World Council of Churches working group meeting in 1956, wrestling with the question of the then recent establishment of Israel, ended its reflections by stating, 'Moreover while we understand the desire of many Jews to have a country of their own, we believe it is their calling to live as the people of God, and not to become merely a nation like others.'[125] Although it may appear in a form that seems relatively benign, the idea that the Jewish people are bound to perpetual movement with no permanent roots in a particular place (unless they wish to forfeit their calling 'to live as the people of God' and 'become merely a nation like others') ultimately stems from the 'teaching of contempt' described in the first chapter, which the Church of England – along with others – now repudiates.

Theology and practice: the ambiguous Abraham

Judaism, Christianity and Islam all respectively consider Abraham to be an ancestor in faith. Indeed in each of these religious traditions the striking description of Abraham as the 'friend' of God is used (Isaiah 41.8; James 2.23; al-Nisa' 4). Yet, in relation to Israel and Palestine, rather than acting as a source for reconciliation all too often the figure of Abraham seems to act as a basis for conflict in the land. Indeed, it is notable how many of the geographical flashpoints in the country seem to have an explicit connection with the stories of Abraham.

A Palestinian Anglican woman, the wife of a priest, herself with Israeli nationality, who had lived both in Israel and in the West Bank, told the story of her encounter with a Western Christian tourist in Jerusalem. On discovering that she was living at the time in the West Bank, the tourist had told her, 'You can't be a real Christian, because if you were a real Christian you would have known that God has given this land to the descendants of Abraham, Isaac and Jacob and you would have got up and left the country!' This was seemingly an allusion to God's covenant with Abraham of land, descendants and nationhood referred to in Genesis, 12, 15 and 17.

However there are also a number of initiatives within Israel itself that link the inspiration for their work to build a shared future for Israel's Jewish and Arab citizens to the figure of 'Abraham'. Most notable of these is perhaps 'the Abraham Fund' whose various initiatives seek 'to fulfill the promise of full and equal citizenship and complete equality of social and political rights for Israel's Jewish and Arab citizens, as embodied in Israel's Declaration of Independence' (Mission Statement; The Abraham Fund, www.abrahamfund.org).

Can the promises to Abraham be read in a way that offers justice to Jews, Christians and Muslims, to Palestinians and to Israelis?

How can the description of Abraham as 'friend of God', common to Judaism, Christianity and Islam, become a resource for peace-building?

Christians have generally understood the promises to Abraham as fulfilled and spiritualized in Jesus Christ. Yet serious Jewish–Christian engagement inevitably forces Christians to address the question as to whether such a reading is the only possible interpretation. What do you think?

6. Ethical Discernment and Common Action

Affirmations

Christians can see in living Jewish traditions of reverence for Torah a love of God and consequent desire to be faithful to God's revealed word. As they seek to be faithful in loving service of the same God, Christians can learn from dialogue with Jews regarding biblical texts and ideas that they share with one another, from their different perspectives. Shared texts, and shared beliefs and values arising from them, enable Christians and Jews to stand, speak and act together, often with others, on issues of public concern in our society, including issues relating to the world as God's creation, the dignity of the human person and freedom of religion, including religious practices of particular value to Christianity or Judaism.

The Introduction to this document opened by stating as its first principle:

● The Christian–Jewish relationship is a gift of God to the Church, which is to be received with care, respect and gratitude, so that we may learn more fully about God's purposes for us and all the world.

In the previous three chapters, the focus has been on theological questions in Christian–Jewish relations that arise from issues that continue to generate tensions: evangelism and conversion, teaching and preaching, and Israel as land and state. With regard to Chapters 3 and 4 in particular, there is the potential for the vestiges of the 'teaching of contempt' about Judaism from previous generations of Christianity to connect with persistent currents of antisemitism within our culture. While addressing the difficult questions that are raised here, these chapters have also sought to show how Christians 'may learn more fully about God's purposes for us and all the world' as they receive with respect and gratitude the 'gift' of the Christian–Jewish relationship.

As will be explored in a moment, the differences between Christianity and Judaism with regard to ethical discernment need to be acknowledged, along with a legacy here too of suspicion and misunderstanding. Yet the common ground between Christians and Jews is evident when it comes to seeking to know the will of God for right action. There is also, therefore, significant opportunity both for Christians to learn from Jewish people about seeking the ways of God, and for Christians and Jews to work and act together on the basis of overlapping (not identical) insights. This final chapter focuses especially on how to receive the gift of the Christian–Jewish relationship.

What does God require of those who seek to be faithful to God's word, and how do we interpret God's word in order to know that? While Christians and Jews look to some common texts that both would regard as Scripture to answer that question, they have done so from divergent perspectives. The place of the Torah given through Moses (usually translated as 'law' in Christian Bibles, though it could also be rendered as 'instruction' or 'teaching') within divine revelation as a whole has been one of the recurring issues here in exchanges between Christians and Jews over two thousand years. For Christians, the books of the Law – the first five books of the biblical canon – are to be read in the light of the teaching of the New Testament about Jesus Christ, and about faith, grace and life in the Spirit. For Jews, the commandments contained in these books of Moses are at the heart of the relationship between Israel and God, with their application to be considered with the benefit of the centuries-long Rabbinic conversation captured in the Midrash, Mishnah and Talmud and then on through Jewish teaching to the present day.[126]

In the polemical exchanges between Christians and Jews in the pre-modern period, Jews criticized Christians for picking and choosing between the commandments of the Law, as if any of the instruction God had given once for all time could be summarily abrogated. Christians criticized Jews for clinging to the letter of the Law when its spiritual fulfilment had been made plain in Christ and in the Church. The teaching of the Protestant Reformers contributed to a sharpening of the distinction between 'law' that will only condemn and 'grace' that alone can save. When Christians began to be aware of the significance of the Talmud and other post-biblical texts for their Jewish contemporaries, they generally took a very negative view of them, arguing that they obstructed a truthful reading of the Scriptures themselves. To some extent, this mirrored the verdict of Jewish scholars on the New Testament.

In the light of welcome developments in Christian–Jewish relations over the last sixty years, as reviewed in earlier chapters of this document, it is important to acknowledge and to reject negative stereotypes that have been current among Christians regarding Jewish attitudes to Law/Torah. For instance, the accusation of 'legalism', with regard to Jewish tradition as a whole in the ancient world (including the time of Jesus) and subsequently, represents an inaccurate and unhelpful misreading of the 'love of the Law/Torah' that is so exuberantly expressed in Psalm 119 and that has been a characteristic feature of Jewish existence.[127] That is not to say that there have never been failures to keep in balance rule and principle, moral imperative and secondary application; but such failures are part of the fallen human condition, and examples can be found among people of all religions and none, including Christians.

With false and simplistic contrasts in this area having been put aside, since the 1960s statements on Christian–Jewish relations from both the Christian and the Jewish side have sought to highlight the shared ethical concerns and overlapping ethical frameworks of the two faiths. For instance, *The Way of Dialogue* asserts:

> Christians and Jews share one hope, which is for the realisation of God's Kingdom on earth. Together they wait for it, pray for it and prepare for it. This Kingdom is nothing less than human life and society transformed, transfigured and transparent to the glory of God.[128]

This eschatological approach to defining the common ethical ground for Christians and Jews reappears in the 1994 document *Christians and Jews*, which moves from the hope that 'the world can be transformed, that it can "be repaired"' to the claim that seeking and praying for the coming of God's kingdom commits Christians and Jews together 'to the task of making the world a more just and more peaceful place; to the proper recognition of the human worth and dignity of every human person'.[129] Similarly, *Sharing One Hope?* comments on the passage cited above from the *Way of Dialogue*:

> On such a basis of shared values, Jews and Christians can work together 'for social justice, respect for the rights of persons and nations, and social and international reconciliation' (Vatican, *Notes*

on *Preaching and Catechesis*, 11). They will also recognize that Muslims, Hindus, Sikhs and members of other faith communities, as well as other people of good will, can in many situations be their partners in this work.[130]

The document does not, however, specify what precisely the 'shared values' are, while as the second sentence implies, these values may well be shared in whole or part with many other people, some religious and some not. Such statements from the Christian side find a significant parallel in the eighth 'word' from *Dabru Emet*:

Jews and Christians must work together for justice and peace. Jews and Christians, each in their own way, recognize the unredeemed state of the world as reflected in the persistence of persecution, poverty, and human degradation and misery. Although justice and peace are finally God's, our joint efforts, together with those of other faith communities, will help bring the kingdom of God for which we hope and long. Separately and together, we must work to bring justice and peace to our world. In this enterprise, we are guided by the vision of the prophets of Israel.[131]

The wording here helpfully emphasizes that for Christians and Jews alike, there is a fundamental relationship between human task and divine gift in ethics: 'justice and peace are finally God's', as is the kingdom for which we pray, yet our 'efforts ... will help bring it' into reality. Moreover, for both there is a powerful ethical vision that follows from doctrinal commitments (for example, 'the unredeemed state of the world', implying a doctrine of redemption), yet the action that follows from this vision can find partners in people who do not share those commitments.[132]

The Way of Dialogue also claimed that Jews, Muslims and Christians 'share a common obligation to love God with their whole being and their neighbours as themselves'. That 'obligation' is based on passages in the New Testament responding to questions about the 'first' or 'greatest' of the commandments in the Law of Moses. The answer combining Deuteronomy 6.4-5 and Leviticus 19.18 is given by Jesus in Mark 12.28-34 and Matthew 22.34-40, though in Luke 10.25 it comes from 'a lawyer', whose response Jesus praises. It is not only the case that Christians and Jews alike read the Law/Torah of Moses alongside the Prophets and the Writings as Holy Scripture. In the New Testament, which Christians juxtapose to these texts, Jesus Christ our teacher comments on the Law of Moses, engages in debate with other Jewish teachers about how to interpret it and proposes two passages that are part of the Law as the hermeneutical key for understanding the whole of the Law and for fulfilling the will of God. The New Testament commits the Church to continuing to hear through the reading and study of the Old Testament the guidance of God for our lives.

What has become known in Christian tradition as 'the Summary of the Law', Jesus' response to the question about the greatest commandment, has found an enduring place within Christian teaching and worship, including contemporary Anglican liturgy, where it is sometimes used to prepare the congregation for prayers of penitence. What is called the first or greatest commandment in the teaching of Jesus has a central role in Jewish liturgy, as the Shema, which may be described as the Jewish credo. Moreover, the Church of England has shared with Rabbinic Judaism a commitment to maintaining a regular pattern of corporate daily prayer, including recitation of psalms within this, with an expectation that participation will be morally formative.

Thus in the Book of Common Prayer, which has shaped the Church of England's worship for nearly half a millennium, the Ten Commandments are to be recited at the beginning of every service of Holy Communion, as a reminder of God's will for our lives and to provide a space for consideration of where we have resisted it. Following medieval Catholic practice and in keeping with some Continental Protestant churches, the Church of England included the memorization of the Ten Commandments as part of its Catechism in the sixteenth century, which all candidates for confirmation were expected to be able to recite. That tradition of making the Ten Commandments one of a handful of basic texts for discipleship is continued in the 'Pilgrim' materials prepared for contemporary use within the Church of England for nurturing and teaching those who are new to the Christian faith.[133]

This sharing of biblical sources for moral formation and deliberation has also been commented on in statements from the Christian side, including documents from the Roman Catholic Church.[134] Yet it is hard to find a straightforward parallel in Christian dialogue texts for the way that *Dabru Emet* builds on its second 'word' to say in its fourth 'word':

Jews and Christians accept the moral principles of Torah.[135] Central to the moral principles of Torah is the inalienable sanctity and dignity of every human being. All of us were created in the image of God. This shared moral emphasis can be the basis of an improved relationship between our two communities. It can also be the basis of a powerful witness to all humanity for improving the lives of our fellow human beings and for standing against the immoralities and idolatries that harm and degrade us. Such witness is especially needed after the unprecedented horrors of the past century.

Anglicans are able to affirm these statements. They can do so for reasons that would be shared by many other Christians as well, including the recognition of every human being as created in the divine image, and the commitment to act towards others in a way that is consistent with that recognition. In the same piece from which this document quoted in its opening paragraphs, Archbishop Justin Welby wrote that 'All humans are made in the image of God. Antisemitism undermines and distorts this truth: it is the negation of God's plan for his creation and is therefore a denial of God himself.'[136] His predecessor, Archbishop Rowan Williams, wrote on visiting Auschwitz-Birkenau in 2008, 'This is a pilgrimage not to a holy place but to a place of utter profanity – a place where the name of God was profaned because the image of God in human beings was abused and disfigured.'[137] In the same year, on visiting the same place, the then Chief Rabbi, Jonathan Sacks, said: 'Here they murdered the image of God that lives in every man, woman and child, and here they tried to silence God himself. The voice that ceaselessly says "Do not murder, do not stand idly by the blood of your neighbour, do not oppress the stranger."'[138] Shared theological teaching provides a shared vision of human life, with its dignity and responsibility, and therefore a shared perspective on human morality.

Anglicans also have significant resources within their own tradition in this context, including the use of the 'Summary of the Law' and the Ten Commandments in liturgical and catechetical contexts. Moreover, Article VII of the Thirty-Nine Articles of Religion of the Church of England affirms that:

> The Old Testament is not contrary to the New: for both in the Old and New Testament everlasting life is offered to Mankind by Christ, who is the only Mediator between God and Man, being both God

and Man. Wherefore they are not to be heard, which feign that the old Fathers did look only for transitory promises. Although the Law given from God by Moses, as touching Ceremonies and Rites, do not bind Christian men, nor the Civil precepts thereof ought of necessity to be received in any commonwealth; yet notwithstanding, no Christian man whatsoever is free from the obedience of the Commandments which are called Moral.

While the distinction appealed to here between ritual, civil and moral commandments is one that could be criticized on a number of grounds, and many Jews would resist its use to confine obedience to certain precepts only, there is a clear assertion being made that the commands of the Law of Moses that relate to moral matters continue to be binding for Christians. The place of the Ten Commandments in the Communion Service of the Book of Common Prayer and in its Catechism shows that it was regarded as belonging in its entirety within this category. The moral character of many of the commandments given to Moses that is asserted here entails that Christian ethics must reckon very carefully with this part of the scriptural witness, alongside others.

One of the formative and most enduringly influential works of Anglican theology, Richard Hooker's *Laws of Ecclesiastical Polity*, begins with a rich exposition of the theology of law, drawing on medieval Catholic thought including that of Thomas Aquinas, which includes a specific place for the divine commandments in Scripture.[139] It also articulates an understanding of natural law that is in continuity with medieval tradition. Continuing common ground between Anglicans and Catholics in this area is discussed in *Life in Christ*, one of the agreed statements of the Anglican–Roman Catholic International Commission, while it has been argued by David Novak, a Jewish scholar, that Christian conceptions of natural law parallel the Jewish idea of the Noahide laws.[140] In both cases, revelation is taken to affirm the existence of moral norms that are available to all, and that people of faith can affirm both to and with those who do not share their faith.

In a context of pressing concerns regarding social and environmental ethics, and where ethical disagreements exercise a deeply polarizing effect within and between societies, Christians and Jews can find significant common ground in dialogue with one another. Texts that both receive as Holy Scripture contain divinely revealed instruction to Israel, which touches on all areas of human life and continues to provide guidance for us today in the everyday challenges of moral living, as well as in reflection on ethical questions featuring in public debate. For both, the Holy Scriptures begin with an account of creation, including the creation of humanity, that should frame our approach in all these situations.

Christian and Jewish communities are both likely in contemporary pluralistic democracies to experience from time to time some tension between the commitments that arise for them from seeking to be faithful to divinely revealed teaching and the expectations of secularizing societies. Here too there are opportunities for them to listen to, learn from and, where appropriate, support one another in the public square.

Traditional Jewish practices around shechita (ritual slaughter) and circumcision have come under criticism in some Western countries in recent decades. While Christians would not consider themselves bound by the relevant commandments from the Old Testament, respect for the texts as divinely inspired Scripture and appreciation of Jewish concern to respond faithfully to divine commands would be significant factors for Christians to consider in engaging with such debates. The role of circumcision in the covenant with Abraham gives it a particular importance in Jewish self-understanding that Christians should also be able to appreciate. While the perceived tensions with other ethical imperatives, not least that of avoiding harm, cannot be simply dismissed, there is a wider question at stake as to whether a secular society must be one in which all abide by secularist morality or can be one that is inherently hospitable to a plurality of religious and non-religious forms of community and belief. Christians and Jews alike will want to advocate the virtues of the latter.[141]

Theology and practice: acting together 'In Good Faith'

'In Good Faith' is a joint initiative of the Archbishop of Canterbury and the UK's Chief Rabbi Ephraim Mirvis that seeks to encourage local partnerships between Anglican priests and Orthodox rabbis. Rooted in the strong friendship between the two leaders, the project particularly focuses on the potential for Christians and Jews to collaborate on social action projects.

Welcoming participants to the launch event at Lambeth Palace in 2016, the Archbishop outlined the values common to Christianity and Judaism, concluding:

> Given that we share this understanding of our society and our place in it, we are in a remarkably strong place to model ground-breaking grassroots relationships which will spawn creative engagement and civic renewal, not only for our places of worship and faith institutions, but also for our whole society ... We are called to pray and to work for the flourishing of the whole of society. The vision and call from God through the prophet Jeremiah to the people in exile in Babylon is our call too. If the people of Britain flourish, then our communities, families, people and we will flourish too. (For a full account, see www.archbishopofcanterbury.org/speaking-and-writing/latest-news/news-archive-2016/archbishop-and-chief-rabbi-launch-rabbis-and.)

While building good working relationships is a long-term endeavour, already a range of positive developments have been reported, such as a project to distribute excess food from Jewish community celebrations via church-hosted food banks, and increased Christian involvement with Mitzvah Day, which promotes social action in Jewish communities. The Council for Christians and Jews has encouraged similar collaboration through its Rabbi/Clergy Action Network, which has members from a range of Christian and Jewish denominations.

What kind of local issues might form a good basis for collaborative social action between Christian and Jews?

What are the obstacles to Jews and Christians working together on social action projects, and how might these be addressed?

An Afterword

'Behold, how good and pleasant it is for brothers to dwell together in unity' (Psalm 133.1).

The sanctity of the occasion was palpable. Standing beside His Grace, Archbishop Justin Welby, each of us absorbed in prayer facing the Kotel – the Western Wall in Jerusalem – was a moment that will for ever remain with me as uniquely powerful and inspiring. I was acutely aware that, however indelible the mark of that experience was upon me personally, far more consequential was the deep, symbolic importance of an Archbishop of Canterbury and Chief Rabbi praying alongside each other in kinship before the remnants of the Holy Temple.

As we prayed, my thoughts turned to the pain that has so often marred the long history of Christian–Jewish relations. It was a moment of genuine healing. How I would love to call out, back through the annals of history, to let my ancestors know that there would be a time of warm friendship between successive Archbishops of Canterbury and Chief Rabbis. For if I could somehow let them know that one day the foremost spiritual leader of the Anglican Church would join a Chief Rabbi in prayer at the Western Wall in a sovereign Jewish State, realizing our two thousand year-long dream of returning to our homeland, they would have simply found it inconceivable.

The symbolism of that special moment will remain with me, and many Jews around the world, long into the future. The deeply rooted connection members of the Jewish faith have with the land of Israel is a fundamental part of who we are, and goes to the heart of our Jewish identity. Praying together beside the last vestiges of the Second Temple, built in 515 BC and destroyed in 70 AD, was a very considerable gesture, and demonstrated a sincere understanding of, in the words of this document, 'the deep and far-reaching relationship between Jewish people and both the land and the State of Israel'.

As for my ancestors, their interaction with Christianity meant being faced with the brutality of the Crusades; it meant being forced to choose between converting to Christianity or certain death; it meant false accusations of sacrificing Christian children at Passover to obtain blood for matzah in what became the cruel Blood Libel; it meant requiring the great Rabbinic leaders, including a figure no less than the Ramban (Nachmanides, 1194–1270), to publicly defend their faith against prominent priests as part of the ignominy of the Disputations, resulting in censorship, violence and slaughter.

Inconceivable. Yet there we were.

There are very rare and special instances when, as Chief Rabbi, one is afforded the tremendous privilege of confronting the sweep of Jewish history and, in turn, an opportunity to make a contribution to it. This was one such time, and I was left in no doubt about the miracle that constitutes the extraordinary distance that Christians and Jews have travelled together, repairing much of our tragic past.

God's Unfailing Word, upon which I am delighted to have had the opportunity to reflect, is sensitive and unequivocal in owning the legacy of Christianity's role in the bitter saga of Jewish persecution.

'Promotion of what has been called "the teaching of contempt" has fostered attitudes of distrust and hostility among Christians towards their Jewish neighbours, in some cases leading to violent attacks, murder and expulsion.'

This is one example among many within a careful exploration of our 'difficult history'. The document's honest appraisal of the destructive nature and origins of Christian perceptions of the Jewish people is brave and welcome and I commend, indeed thank, the Church of England for its willingness to engage in this moving act of self-reflection.

I must, though, convey a substantial misgiving I have with this document, despite the progress it undeniably represents and articulates. Namely, that it does not reject the efforts of those Christians, however many they may number, who, as part of their faithful mission, dedicate themselves to the purposeful and specific targeting of Jews for conversion to Christianity.

In 2015, the Vatican issued a document exploring 'theological questions pertaining to Catholic–Jewish Relations'. In doing so, it took the opportunity to make clear that the Catholic Church would 'neither conduct nor support any specific institutional mission work directed towards Jews'. This represented a major theological step forward, which was warmly welcomed across the Jewish world.

The enduring existence within the Anglican Church of a theological approach that is permissive of this behaviour does considerable damage to the relationship between our faith traditions, and, consequently, pursuing a comprehensive new Christian–Jewish paradigm in this context is exceptionally challenging. It is as though we are jointly building an essential new structure, while simultaneously a small part of the construction team is deliberately destabilizing the building's very foundations, thereby undermining confidence in the structural integrity of the whole edifice.

The real impact of this upon prospective Jewish participants in our interfaith dialogue is, inevitably, to diminish the basis of trust that is so integral to the relationship. Any suspicion that our engagement is being directed by a purpose other than the betterment of our mutual understanding and a necessary contribution to the common good is harmful and takes us sharply backwards. This is quite apart from the more obvious problem: the affront to our fundamental right to the integrity of Jewish self-definition.

We are left, therefore, with two apparently contradictory narratives: one represented by that glorious day in Jerusalem with my friend, the Archbishop, further to the dramatic transformation of the relationship between our great faiths, which made that possible. The other, a real and persistent concern, set in a tragic historical context, that even now, in the twenty-first Century, Jews are seen by some as quarry to be pursued and converted.

These contradictory narratives challenge us. We must acknowledge the strain this places on the credibility of our endeavour, and, despite the incongruity, we absolutely must persist with energy and a sense of resolute hope in our attempts to move forward in harmony.

Where there is profound friendship, as there is here, there must be honesty, even when what is said by one friend in addressing the other might well be received as being disagreeable. There can be no other way. I offer these reflections to you, our Christian brothers and sisters, entirely in that spirit. The importance of doing so is inextricably linked to the need to bear witness to the calamities of our past in a way that is just and true. More important still is the way that it impacts our conception of each other and the future we can create together, so that we may, in our fundamentally different but connected ways, be a source of immense blessing to our world.

Chief Rabbi Ephraim Mirvis

Notes

1   Justin Welby, 'Vigilance and Resolution: Living Antidotes to an Ancient Virus', in *Lessons Learned? Reflections on Antisemitism and the Holocaust*, from the Holocaust Educational Trust and The Community Security Trust (2016), p. 10; available at www.het.org.uk/images/downloads/Lessons-Learned-HET-CST.pdf (accessed 22/03/19).

2   The wording is taken from the Declaration of Assent made by all clergy of the Church of England at ordination and at subsequent licensing to office, as set out in Canon C 15; available at www.churchofengland.org/more/policy-and-thinking/canons-church-england/section-c (accessed 22/03/2019).

3   Rather than seeking to use a single 'neutral' term such as 'Hebrew Bible', this document uses 'Old Testament' when speaking in the context of Christian Scripture, 'Tanakh' when speaking in the context of Jewish Scripture, and 'Old Testament/Tanakh' when speaking in the context of Scripture as shared by Christians and Jews.

4   Christians should have some awareness of the diversity within Judaism. This includes the various religious traditions within Judaism, e.g. Orthodox, Reform, Liberal, Hasidic, Masorti. Judaism is, however, a people as well as a religion, and there are many Jewish people who do not observe religious customs or subscribe to religious beliefs. While there are important questions that may be asked about how Judaism is defined, Christians need to attend to the answers given by Jewish people themselves.

5   Quoted in James K. Aitken and Edward Kessler (eds), *Challenges in Jewish–Christian Relations* (New York: Paulist Press, 2006). Research is currently being undertaken into the correspondence of the Revd James Parkes with Archbishop William Temple held at the Parkes Institute Library at Southampton University regarding the views on Judaism held by the Archbishop himself.

6   The Council of Christians and Jews website is at www.ccj.org.uk/.

7   For the text of the report as published by the Anglican Consultative Council (ACC) after the Conference, see *Jews, Christians and Muslims: The Way of Dialogue*, Appendix 6 in *The Truth Shall Make You Free: The Lambeth Conference 1988, Reports, Resolutions and Pastoral Letters from the Bishops* (London: Anglican Consultative Council, 1988); also available at http://nifcon.anglicancommunion.org/media/129614/lam88_ap6.pdf (accessed 22/03/2019). The full text of Resolution 21 on 'Interfaith Dialogue: Christian/Jewish/Muslim from the 1988 Conference can be found at www.anglicancommunion.org/media/127749/1988.pdf (accessed 22/03/2019).

8   See the brief account of Richard Harries, *After the Evil: Christianity and Judaism in the Shadow of the Holocaust* (Oxford: Oxford University Press, 2003), pp. 3–5.

9   Churches' Commission for Inter Faith Relations, *Christians and Jews: A New Way of Thinking – Guidelines for the Churches* (London: Churches Together in Britain and Ireland, 1994), p. 2.

10   Inter Faith Consultative Group of the Archbishops' Council, *Sharing One Hope? The Church of England and Christian–Jewish Relations: A Contribution to a Continuing Debate* (London: Church House Publishing, 2001), p. 37.

11   Anglican Communion Network for Inter Faith Concerns, *Generous Love: The Truth of the Gospel and the Call to Dialogue. An Anglican Theology of Inter Faith Relations* (London: Anglican Consultative Council, 2008); also available at https://nifcon. anglicancommunion.org/media/18910/generous_love_a4_with_foreward.pdf (accessed 25/03/2019). The work of the Network is now being continued by the Anglican Inter Faith Commission.

12   Anglican Communion's Network for Inter Faith Concerns (NIFCON), *Land of Promise? An Anglican Exploration of Christian Attitudes to the Holy Land, with Special Reference to 'Christian Zionism', 2012*, available at www.anglicancommunion.org/media/ 39759/land_of_promise.pdf (accessed 25/03/2019).

13   Sources of information include the All Party Parliamentary Group Against Antisemitism, the Community Security Trust (CST) and the Shami Chakrabarti Inquiry (into allegations of antisemitism in the Labour Party).

14   Cf. L. Daniel Staetsky, *Antisemitism in Contemporary Great Britain: A Study of Attitudes towards Jews and Israel* (London: Institute for Jewish Policy Research (IJPR), 2017), p. 6; available at http://archive.jpr.org.uk/object-uk450 (accessed 25/03/2019).

15   'Palestine' is used here in accordance with common academic practice when writing about the period of Roman occupation.

16   George Brooke, *The Dead Sea Scrolls and the New Testament* (London: SPCK, 2005); Susan Docherty, *The Jewish Pseudepigrapha: An Introduction* (London: SPCK, 2014); Jodi Magness, *The Archaeology of the Holy Land from the Destruction of Solomon's Temple to the Muslim Conquest* (New York: Cambridge University Press, 2012); Jodi Magness, *Stone and Dung, Oil and Spit: Jewish Daily Life in the Time of Jesus* (Grand Rapids: Eerdmans, 2011).

17.   James Dunn, *The Partings of the Ways between Judaism and Christianity and their Significance for the Character of Christianity* (London: SCM Press, 1991). Since Dunn published his study, a great deal of further research into this question has been published, including: Adam Becker and Annette Yoshiko Reed (eds), *The Ways that Never Parted: Jews and Christians in Late Antiquity and the Early Middle Ages* (Minneapolis: Fortress Press, 2007); Daniel Boyarin, *Border Lines: The Partition of Judaeo-Christianity* (Philadelphia: University of Pennsylvania Press, 2004); Paula Fredriksen, 'Mandatory Retirement: Ideas in the Study of Christian Origins Whose Time has Come to Go', in David B. Capes, April D. DeConick and Helen K. Bond (eds),

Israel's God and Rebecca's Children: Christology and Community in Early Judaism and Christianity: Essays in Honor of Larry W. Hurtado and Alan F. Segal (Waco, TX: Baylor University Press, 2007), pp. 25–38; Andrew Jacobs, 'Jews and Christians', in Susan Ashbrook Harvey and David G. Hunter (eds), *Oxford Handbook of Early Christian Studies* (Oxford: Oxford University Press, 2008), pp. 169–85; Judith M. Lieu, *Neither Jew nor Greek? Constructing Early Christianity* (London: T&T Clark, 2002); Anders Runesson, 'Inventing Christian Identity: Paul, Ignatius, and Theodosius I', in Bengt Holmberg (ed.), *Exploring Early Christian Identity*, Wissenschaftliche Untersuchungen zum Neuen Testament vol. 226 (Tübingen: Mohr Siebeck, 2008), pp. 59–92; Leonard V. Rutgers, *Making Myths: Jews in Early Christian Identity Formation* (Leuven: Peeters, 2009).

18 D. Cohn-Sherbok, *Messianic Judaism* (London: Continuum, 2000); Oskar Skarsaune and Reidar Hvalvik, *Jewish Believers in Jesus: The Early Centuries* (Peabody, MA: Hendrickson, 2007); *Sharing One Hope?*, chapter 6, 'Jewish People who Believe in Jesus', and Appendix 2, 'Messianic Congregations and Traditional Churches'.

19 Israel Yuval, *Two Nations in Your Womb: Perceptions of Jews and Christians in Late Antiquity and the Middle Ages* (Berkeley: University of California Press, 2006); Jonathan Elukin, *Living Together, Living Apart: Rethinking Jewish–Christian Relations in the Middle Ages* (Princeton: Princeton University Press, 2007).

20 Yehuda Liebes, *Studies in the Zohar* (Albany: SUNY Press, 1993); Peter Schäfer, *Mirror of His Beauty: Feminine Images of God from the Bible to the Early Kabbalah* (Princeton: Princeton University Press, 2004).

21 Christians refer to the 'sacrifice', Jews to the 'binding' of Isaac. For the interaction of the two traditions, see Edward Kessler, *Bound by the Bible: Jews, Christians and the Sacrifice of Isaac* (Cambridge: Cambridge University Press, 2004).

22 Michael Hilton, *The Christian Effect on Jewish Life* (London: SCM Press, 1994); Jeremy F. Worthen, *The Internal Foe: Judaism and Anti-Judaism in the Shaping of Christian Theology* (Newcastle: Scholars Press, 2009); Daniel R. Langton, *The Apostle Paul in the Jewish Imagination: A Study in Modern Jewish–Christian Relations* (Cambridge: Cambridge University Press, 2010).

23 David Daniell, *The Bible in English: Its History and Influence* (New Haven: Yale University Press, 2003). Christian use of Jewish biblical scholarship goes all the way back to Jerome (347–420). In the late Middle Ages it was characteristic of Franciscan Bible commentators such as Nicholas of Lyra. See Deeana Copeland Klepper, *The Insight of Unbelievers: Nicholas of Lyra and Christian Reading of Jewish Text in the Later Middle Ages* (Philadelphia: University of Pennsylvania Press, 2007).

24 *The Mishnah*, translated by H. Danby (Oxford: Clarendon Press, 1933).

25 By Moritz Steinschneider, in response to the French writer Ernest Renan who had written about the inferiority of the 'Semitic race', and whom he accused of *antisemitische Vorurteile* (antisemitic prejudices). See e.g. Alex Bein, *The Jewish Question: Bibliography of a World Problem*, trans. Harry Zohn (Rutherford, NJ: Fairleigh Dickinson University Press, 1990), p. 594.

26 See the announcement from the International Holocaust Remembrance Alliance (IHRA) in May 2016, available at https://holocaustremembrance.com/media-room/stories/working-definition-antisemitism (accessed 25/03/2019).

27 Robert S. Wistrich, *The Longest Hatred* (New York: Schocken, 1994); cf. the earlier work of Edward H. Flannery, *The Anguish of the Jews: Twenty-three Centuries of Anti-Semitism* (New York: MacMillan, 1965).

28 The Aegyptiaca survives only in quotations in other ancient authors, such as the Jewish historian Josephus. For the texts, see Menaham Stern, *Greek and Latin Authors on Jews and Judaism*, vol. 1 (Jerusalem: Israel Academy of Sciences and Humanities, 1994), pp. 62–8. Further: Peter Schäfer, *Judeophobia: Attitudes towards Jews in the Ancient World* (Cambridge, MA: Harvard University Press, 1998).

29 Rosemary Radford Ruether, in her seminal book *Faith and Fratricide: The Christian Roots of Anti-Semitism* (New York: Seabury Press, 1974), argued that 'high' Christology inevitably generated antisemitism.

30 See, for example: Rosemary Radford Ruether, *To Change the World: Christology and Cultural Criticism* (New York: Crossroad, 1983), pp. 31–3; Dan Cohn-Sherbok, *The Crucified Jew: Twenty Centuries of Christian Antisemitism* (London: Fount, 1993), pp. 12–15.

31 Marc Saperstein, *Moments of Crisis in Jewish–Christian Relations* (London: SCM Press, 1989), pp. 27–31; Rowan Williams, *Teresa of Avila* (London: Continuum, 2003), pp. 15–24.

32 For an overview of Luther's statements about Jews and Judaism, see Lyndal Roper, *Martin Luther: Renegade and Prophet* (London: Bodley Head, 2016), pp. 389–96. The influence of the document *Shem Hamephoras* is also significant here, summarized in Frederick M. Schweitzer, 'The Taproot of Antisemitism: The demonization of the Jews', in *Remembering the Future*, vol. 1, *Jews and Christians during and after the Holocaust*, ed. Yehuda Bauer et al. (Oxford: Pergamon Press, 1989), pp. 879–90. See also Richard Harvey, *Luther and the Jews: Putting Right the Lies* (Oregon: Cascade, 2017).

33 Two examples are given in the 'Theology and practice' reflection at the end of this chapter, both discussed in Gavin I. Langmuir, *History, Religion, and Antisemitism*

(Berkeley: University of California Press, 1990). The 'blood libel' survived in some places into the twentieth century, featuring for instance in the history of the Kielce pogrom in Poland in 1946.

34 Jules Isaac, *The Teaching of Contempt* (New York: Holt, Rhinehart and Winston, 1964), pp. 21–4.

35 The work of the American Presbyterian George Foot Moore (1851–1931) and of the Revd James Parkes from the Church of England (1896–1981) was very significant in laying foundations for a change in approach to biblical understanding and to contemporary relations.

36 The more familiar term 'Holocaust' is used in this document rather than 'Shoah'. For a brief discussion of the different shades of meaning between these terms, see the Yad Vashem website, www.yadvashem.org/yv/en/holocaust/resource_center/the_ holocaust.asp (accessed 25/03/2019).

37 Colin Richmond, *Campaigner against Antisemitism: The Reverend James Parkes 1896– 1981* (London: Valentine Mitchell, 2005).

38 Worthen, *Internal Foe*, pp. 174–202. On the debate over the evaluation of Bonhoeffer in this regard, see Stephen R. Haynes, *The Bonhoeffer Legacy: Post–Holocaust Perspectives* (Minneapolis: Fortress Press, 2006); on Barth, George Hunsinger (ed.), *Karl Barth: Post-Holocaust Theologian?* (London: Bloomsbury T&T Clark, 2018); and on Maritain, Robert Royal (ed.), *Jacques Maritain and the Jews* (Mishawaka: American Maritain Association, 1994). De Lubac provided his own account of this period in *Christian Resistance to Anti-Semitism: Memories from 1940–1944*, trans. Elizabeth Englund (San Francisco: Ignatius, 1990).

39 Karl Barth, *Dogmatics in Outline*, trans. G. T. Thomson (London: SCM Press, 1949), pp. 74–5. Barth's approach is set out much more extensively in an earlier work, *Church Dogmatics*, II/2, trans. G. W. Bromiley et al. (Edinburgh: T&T Clark, 1957), §34, 'The Election of the Community', pp. 195–305.

40 See the 'Historical Note' in the 1988 statement from the ecumenical Consultation on the Church and the Jewish People, 'The Churches and the Jewish People: Towards a New Understanding', available at www.jcrelations.net/The+Churches+and+the+ Jewish+People%3A+Toward+a+New+Understanding. 1512.0.html?L=3 (accessed 25/03/2019).

41 The text may be found in Franklin Sherman (ed.), *Bridges: Documents of the Christian– Jewish Dialogue*, vol. 1, *The Road to Reconciliation (1945–1985)* (New York: Paulist Press, 2011), p. 52.

42   Vatican II, *Nostra Aetate*, Declaration on the Relation of the Church to Non-Christian Religions, 1965, no. 4; text available at www.vatican.va/archive/hist_councils/ii_vatican_council/documents/vat-ii_decl_19651028_nostra-aetate_en.html (accessed 25/03/2019).

43   See the list of documents on the web page for the Commission for Religious Relations with the Jews, at www.vatican.va/roman_curia/pontifical_councils/chrstuni/sub-index/index_relations-jews.htm (accessed 25/03/2019).

44   Michael Ramsey, 'Statement by the Archbishop of Canterbury issued from Lambeth Palace on 18 March 1964', printed as Appendix 1 in Peter Schneider, *Sweeter than Honey: Christian Presence amid Judaism* (London: SCM Press, 1966) p.179.

45   See for example R. K. Soulen, *The God of Israel and Christian Theology* (Minneapolis: Augsburg Fortress Press, 1996; Bruce Marshall, 'Christ and the Cultures: The Jewish People in Christian Theology', in *The Cambridge Companion to Christian Doctrine* (Cambridge: Cambridge University Press, 1996), pp. 81–100; Matthew Tapie, *Aquinas on Israel and the Church: The Question of Supersessionism in the Theology of Thomas Aquinas* (Cambridge: James Clarke & Co., 2014). Precise definition is, however, difficult, while others – perhaps most notably the Jewish theologian David Novak – have argued that (a) the claim that certain aspects of Jewish life as it was in the first century AD have been 'superseded' by what God has done in Jesus Christ is in fact integral to Christian faith, and (b) that this claim in some – not all – forms need not prevent mutual respect and dialogue between Christians and Jews. See for instance David Novak, *Talking with Christians: Musings of a Jewish Theologian* (Grand Rapids: Eerdmans, 2005), p. 164.

46   ACC, *Jews, Christians and Muslims*, paragraph 16. The version of the Bible cited is the NEB.

47   Faith and Order Commission, *Forgiveness and Reconciliation in the Aftermath of Abuse* (London: Church House Publishing, 2017), pp. 54–64. See also Jeremy Bergen, *Ecclesial Repentance: The Churches Confront their Sinful Pasts* (London: T&T Clark, 2011).

48   William Horbury, *Jewish Messianism and the Cult of Christ* (London: SCM Press, 1998); Horbury, *Messianism among Jews and Christians* (London/New York: T&T Clark, 2003); Matthew V. Novenson, *The Grammar of Messianism: An Ancient Jewish Political Idiom* (New York: Oxford University Press, 2017).

49   Richard Hays, *Echoes of Scripture in the Gospels and Echoes of Scripture in Paul* (New Haven: Yale University Press, 1989).

50 Judith Lieu, *Marcion and the Making of a Heretic: God and Scripture in the Second Century* (Cambridge: Cambridge University Press, 2015), pp. 398–432. For an accessible account of the continuing dangers for Christian belief in this area, see Angela Tilby's chapter on the heresy of Marcionism in *Heresies and How to Avoid Them*, ed. Ben Quash and Michael Ward (London: SPCK, 2007), pp. 73–80.

51 On this question, see the Commission for Religious Relations with the Jewish People, 'Notes on the Correct Way to Present the Jews and Judaism in Preaching and Catechesis in the Roman Catholic Church', 1985, available at: http://www.vatican.va/roman_curia/pontifical_councils/chrstuni/relations-jews-docs/rc_pc_chrstuni_doc_19820306_jews-judaism_en.html (accessed 25/03/2019).

52 See for instance Article VI of The Thirty-Nine Articles of Religion of the Church of England.

53 See the discussion of Soulen in *God of Israel*, pp. 57–80, and Worthen, *Internal Foe*, pp. 159–65.

54 N. T. Wright, *The Climax of the Covenant: Christ and the Law in Pauline Theology* (Edinburgh: T&T Clark, 1991). See also Alex Jacob, *The Case for Enlargement Theology* (Saffron Walden: Glory to Glory, 2010).

55 As well as Romans 11.1, see e.g. 2 Corinthians 11.22, Philippians 3.4-6 and Acts 21-22.

56 John M.G. Barclay, *Paul and the Gift*, (Grand Rapids, Michigan: Eerdmans, 2015).

57 Robert Davidson and A. R. C. Leaney, *Biblical Criticism*, vol. 3 of *The Pelican Guide to Modern Theology,* ed. R. P. C. Hanson (Harmondsworth: Penguin, 1970), p. 157.

58 See Harold Attridge, *The Epistle to the Hebrews: A Commentary on the Epistle to the Hebrews* (Theology, ed. Philadelphia: Fortress Press, 1989); Richard Hays, '"Here We Have No Lasting City": New Covenantalism in Hebrews' in *The Epistle to the Hebrews and Christian Theology* (ed.), Richard Bauckham et. al. (Grand Rapids: Eerdmans, 2009), pp. 151–73; Luke Timothy Johnson, *Hebrews: A Commentary* (Louisville: Westminster John Knox Press, 2006); Lloyd Kim, *Polemic in the Book of Hebrews: Anti-Judaism, Anti-Semitism, or Supersessionism?* (Eugene, OR: Pickwick Publications, 2006); Andrew Lincoln, *Hebrews: A Guide* (London: T&T Clark, 2006); Alan C. Mitchell, '"A Sacrifice of Praise": Does Hebrews Promote Supersessionism?' in *Reading the Epistle to the Hebrews: A Resource for Students* (ed.), Eric F. Mason and Kevin B. McCruden (Atlanta: Society of Biblical Literature, 2011), pp. 251–67; David Moffitt, *Atonement and the Logic of Resurrection in Hebrews* (Leiden: Brill, 2011). See also Pamela Eisenbaum in the note below.

59   Pamela M. Eisenbaum, 'Hebrews, Supersessionism and Jewish–Christian Relations', presented at the Society of Biblical Literature Annual Meeting (2005), p. 5. Available at www.hebrews.unibas.ch/documents/2005Eisenbaum.pdf (accessed 25/03/2019).

60   See the 12 contributions responding to the question, 'Is there a Special Relationship between Christianity and Judaism?', *Current Dialogue* 58 (2016), pp. 12–64.

61   Vatican II, *Nostra Aetate*, no. 4.

62   Alberto Melloni, '*Nostra Aetate* and the Discovery of the Sacrament of Otherness', in *The Catholic Church and the Jewish People: Recent Reflections from Rome*, ed. Philip A. Cunningham, Norbert J. Hofmann and Joseph Sievers (New York: Fordham University Press, 2007), pp. 150–1.

63   Walter Cardinal Kasper, 'Address on the 37th Anniversary of *Nostra Aetate*', given 28 October, 2002, available at www.ccjr.us/dialogika-resources/documents-and-statements/roman-catholic/kasper/wk02oct28 (accessed 16/04/2019).

64   ACC, *Jews, Christians and Muslims*, paragraphs 13 and 16.

65   Jesper Svartvik, 'Christological and Soteriological Reflections in the Wake of Half a Century of Intense and Improved Jewish–Christian Relations', *Current Dialogue* 44 (December 2004), available at http://wcc-coe.org/wcc/what/interreligious/cd44-12.html (accessed 11/04/2019).

66   On the Augustinian tradition, see, e.g., Jeremy Cohen, *Living Letters of the Law: Ideas of the Jew in Medieval Christianity* (Berkeley, CA: University of California Press, 1999), and on Augustine's own views, Paula Fredriksen, *Augustine and the Jews: A Christian Defense of Jews and Judaism* (New York: Doubleday, 2008).

67   Augustine, *Enarrationes in Psalmos*, 56.9, CCSL 39: 700.

68   Augustine, *Sermo* 5.5, CCSL 41:56.

69   For a detailed and careful study of the tradition, which traces the interaction of Christian attitudes to Jewish people and the development of Christian theology in the medieval period in particular, see Worthen, *Internal Foe.*

70   Bernard, *Epistle 363*. On Bernard's ambiguous attitude to the Jews, see David Berger, 'The Attitude of St Bernard of Clairvaux toward the Jews', *Proceedings of the American Academy for Jewish Research* 40 (1972), pp. 89–108.

71   Vatican II, *Nostra Aetate*, no. 4: 'The Jews should not be spoken of as rejected or accursed … Indeed the church reproves every form of persecution against whomsoever it may be directed … it deplores all hatreds, persecutions, displays of anti-Semitism directed against the Jews at any time or from any source.'

72 Anglican Communion Network for Interfaith Concerns, *Generous Love: The Truth of the Gospel and the Call to Dialogue* (London: ACC, 2008), repeats statements from ACC, *Jews, Christians and Muslims* quoted at p.xx above, adding: 'we need to recognise the continuing vitality of Jewish life and religion over the last two millennia' (p. 5).

73 Svartvik, 'Christological and Soteriological Reflections'.

74 Michael Barnes, *Theology and the Dialogue of Religions* (Cambridge: Cambridge University Press, 2002), p. 62, referring de Michel de Certeau, *The Writing of History* (New York: Columbia University Press, 1988): 'The Jewish other is always returning, always present, "haunting" the space carved out by the dominant Christian "same".'

75 See the dedicated page on the Anglican Communion website, www.anglicancommunion.org/mission/marks-of-mission.aspx

76 ACC, *Jews, Christians and Muslims*, paragraph 27.

77 Reuven Silverman, Patrick Morrow and Daniel Langton, *Jews and Christians: Perspectives on Mission. The Lambeth-Jewish Forum* (Cambridge: Woolf Institute, 2011).

78 According to the statement by the Christian Scholars Group on Christian–Jewish Relations of 1 September 2002, 'A Sacred Obligation', 'In view of our conviction that Jews are in an eternal covenant with God, we renounce missionary efforts directed at converting Jews. At the same time, we welcome opportunities for Jews and Christians to bear witness to their respective experiences of God's saving ways'; see *Seeing Judaism Anew: Christianity's Sacred Obligation,* ed. Mary C. Boys (Lanham, MD: Rowman & Littlefield, 2015), p. xvi.

79 Cf. the Commission for Religious Relations with the Jews, in *'The Gifts and Calling of God are Irrevocable' (Romans 11:29): Reflections on Theological Questions Pertaining to Catholic–Jewish Relations on the Occasion of the 50th Anniversary of Nostra Aetate* (2015), available at www.vatican.va/roman_curia/pontifical_councils/chrstuni/relations-jews-docs/rc_pc_chrstuni_doc_20151210_ebraismo-nostra-aetate_en.html (accessed 16/04/2019). 'The Church is therefore obliged to view evangelisation to Jews, who believe in the one God, in a different manner from that to people of other religions and worldviews. In concrete terms this means that the Catholic Church neither conducts nor supports any specific institutional mission work directed towards Jews. While there is a principled rejection of an institutional mission, Christians are nonetheless called to bear witness to their faith in Jesus Christ also to Jews, although they should do so in a humble and sensitive manner, acknowledging that Jews are bearers of God's Word, and particularly in view of the great tragedy of the Shoah' (no. 40).

80   The text of the Resolutions from the 1978 Lambeth Conference may be found at www.anglicancommunion.org/media/127746/1978.pdf (accessed 16/04/2019).

81   Resolution 16 of the 1897 Lambeth Conference; text at www.anglicancommunion.org/resources/document-library/lambeth-conference/1897/resolution-16.aspx (accessed 16/04/2019).

82   Text in Sherman (ed.), *Bridges*, vol, 1, pp. 47–51.

83   Text in Sherman (ed.), *Bridges*, vol, 1, p. 56.

84   Cf. Article XVIII of the Thirty-Nine Articles of Religion of the Church of England.

85   Christians will receive the challenge from Jews that the Messianic promise of peace and justice has yet to be realized. See, for example, Isaiah 2.1-4 and the emblematic Messianic promise that 'they will beat their swords into ploughshares' (v. 4).

86   See note 17 above for some of the literature on this subject.

87   Cf. *Sharing One Hope?*, chapter 6, 'Jewish People who Believe in Jesus', and Appendix 2, 'Messianic Congregations and Traditional Churches'. There is a growing number of studies in this area, including Richard Harvey, *Mapping Messianic Jewish Theology: A Constructive Approach* (Carlisle: Paternoster, 2009); Mark S. Kinzer, *Postmissionary Messianic Judaism, (*Grand Rapids, MI: Brazos Press, 2005); Mark S. Kinzer, *Searching Her Own Mystery: Nostra Aetate, the Jewish People, and the Identity of the Church* (Eugene OR: Cascade, 2015); David J. Rudolph and Joel Willitts, *Introduction to Messianic Judaism: Its Ecclesial Context and Biblical Foundations* (Grand Rapids: Zondervan, 2013).

88   Commission for Religious Relations with Jews, *Notes on the Correct Way to Present Jews and Judaism in Preaching and Catechesis of the Roman Catholic Church* (1985), e.g. section 1, paragraph 8: 'The urgency and importance of precise, objective and rigorously accurate teaching on Judaism for our faithful follows too from the danger of anti-Semitism which is always ready to reappear under different guises. The question is not merely to uproot from among the faithful the remains of anti-Semitism still to be found here and there, but much rather to arouse in them, through educational work, an exact knowledge of the wholly unique "bond" which joins us as a Church to the Jews and to Judaism. In this way, they would learn to appreciate and love the latter, who have been chosen by God to prepare the coming of Christ and have preserved everything that was progressively revealed and given in the course of that preparation, notwithstanding their difficulty in recognising in Him their Messiah.' Text available at www.vatican.va/roman_curia/pontifical_councils/chrstuni/relations-jews-docs/rc_pc_chrstuni_doc_19820306_jews-judaism_en.html (accessed 16/04/2019).

89   World Council of Churches, 'Ecumenical Considerations on Jewish–Christian Dialogue' (1982), available at www.oikoumene.org/en/resources/documents/wccprogrammes/interreligious-dialogue-and-cooperation/interreligious-trust-and-respect/ecumenical-considerations-on-jewish-christian-dialogue (accessed 16/04/2019). Amy-Jill Levine and Marc Zvi Brettler (ed.), *The Jewish Annotated New Testament*, 2nd edition (Oxford: Oxford University Press, 2017) identifies a list of common errors often made in Christian teaching and preaching.

90   Inter Faith Consultative Group of the Archbishops' Council, *Sharing One Hope?*, p 30.

91   Archbishops' Council, *Common Worship: Times and Seasons* (London: Church House Publishing, 2006), p. 259.

92   See Marilyn J. Salmon, *Preaching Without Contempt: Overcoming Unintended Anti-Judaism* (Minneapolis, MN: Augsburg Fortress, 2006); Ann Conway-Jones, 'Contempt or Respect? Jews and Judaism in Christian Preaching', *Expository Times* 127:2 (2015), pp. 63–72.

93   E.g. Amy-Jill Levine, *Short Stories by Jesus: The Enigmatic Parables of a Controversial Rabbi* (London: HarperCollins, 2015); Kenneth E. Bailey, *Jesus through Middle Eastern Eyes: Cultural Studies in the Gospels* (London: SPCK, 2008).

94   Malcolm Lowe, 'Who Were the ΙΟΥΔΑΙΟΙ?', *Novum Testamentum* 18:2 (1976), pp. 101-30, DOI: 10.2307/1560764, available at www.jstor.org/stable/i270203 (accessed 16/04/2019).

95   See: Steve Mason, 'Jews, Judaeans, Judaizing, Judaism: Problems of Categorization in Ancient History', *Journal for the Study of Judaism* 38:4 (2007), pp. 457–512; David M. Miller, 'Ethnicity, Religion and the Meaning of Ioudaios in Ancient "Judaism"', *Currents in Biblical Research* 12:2 (2014), pp. 216–65; Timothy Michael Law and Charles Halton (eds), '*Jew and Judean: A MARGINALIA Forum on Politics and Historiography in the Translation of Ancient Texts*' (The Marginalia Review of Books, 2014, http://marginalia.lareviewofbooks.org/jew-judean-forum/(accessed 16/04/2019).

96   Adele Reinhartz, 'Judaism in the Gospel of John', *Interpretation* 63:4 (2009), pp. 382–93.

97   Jeremy Worthen, 'Difficult Texts: Matthew 27.25', *Theology* 118:5 (2015), pp. 354–56.

98   Michael Ramsey, 'Statement by the Archbishop of Canterbury'.

99   The forthcoming commentary by Jonathan Wittenberg on the Synagogue lectionary will be a useful source for Christian preachers who would like to learn from Jewish perspectives on passages they will be expounding.

100 Another example – also from a hymn associated with Advent – would be 'O Come, O Come, Emmanuel', with its opening plea to God to 'ransom captive Israel', potentially invoking the image of blinded and defeated Synagoga as presented in the discussion panel at the end of Chapter 2, though, again, it will seem natural to many Christians to identify themselves here with Israel crying out for God's deliverance. Some hymn books make changes to the wording in these and other texts to address concerns about antisemitism and anti-Judaism.

101 There is much material to assist teachers and preachers in this regard in Levine and Brettler (eds.), *Jewish* Annotated New Testament.

102 Michael Hilton, *The Christian Effect on Jewish Life* (London: SCM Press, 1994), pp. 33–4.

103 Phrase taken from the Declaration of Independence of the State of Israel, May 1948. For an overview of the variety of perspectives among different Jewish and Christian groups on the Land and the State of Israel, see Daniel R. Langton, *Children of Zion: Jewish and Christian Perspectives on the Holy Land* (Cambridge: Woolf Institute of Abrahamic Faiths, 2008), written under the auspices of the Lambeth Jewish Forum. The ambiguity of what it means to be a Jew, a word that expresses both religious and also ethnic identity, adds additional complications to any discussion of this issue; see note 4 above.

104 The national anthem of Israel 'Hatikva' = *The Hope,* speaks of the Jewish hope over two thousand years to be 'a free people in our own land'.

105 The term 'Zionism' was first used by Nathan Birnbaum in Vienna in 1880, in the periodical *Selbstemanzipation!*

106 Anglican Communion's Network for Inter Faith Concerns (NIFCON), *Land of Promise?* p. 4.

107 The Jewish Autonomous Region established in eastern Russia by the Soviet Union in 1928 might also be noted in this regard, though Jews today constitute a very small minority of the population.

108 See Donald Lewis, *The Origins of Christian Zionism: Lord Shaftesbury and Evangelical Support for a Jewish Homeland* (Cambridge: Cambridge University Press, 2010); Andrew Crome, *Christian Zionism and English Identity, 1600–1850* (Basingstoke: Palgrave Macmillan, 2018). Note, for example, how Charles Wesley's hymn 'Almighty God of Love', based on texts from Isaiah 66 and Romans 11, looks forward to the restoration of the Jewish people to the land of Israel. It was first published by his brother John in *Short Hymns on Select Passages of the Holy Scriptures* in 1762, and it continued to appear in Methodist hymnbooks at least till the twentieth century. The role of Christian Restorationism in the eventual founding of the State of Israel has been virtually written

out of Zionist historiography, but it was well recognized by earlier Zionists: see Nahum Sokolow, *History of Zionism 1600–1918*, 2 vols (London: Longman's, Green & Co., 1919).

109 See Philip Alexander, 'Why did Lord Balfour Back the Balfour Declaration?' *Jewish Historical Studies* 49:10 (2018), pp. 188–214; Roger Spooner, 'Evangelicals, the Balfour Declaration and Zionism', on the Balfour Project available at www.balfourproject.org/evangelicals-the-balfour-declaration-and-zionism/ (accessed 16/04/2019).

110 Thus support of Israel by Christians simply because of the horror of the Holocaust or the fact that the State of Israel was established by a UN resolution in 1947 would not be considered Christian Zionism.

111 The Anglican Consultative Council, Resolution 15.32: Land of Promise?, available at www.anglicancommunion.org/structures/instruments-of-communion/acc/acc-15/resolutions.aspx#s32 accessed (16/04/2019).

112 For Darby's historical background, see Donald H. Akenson, *Discovering the End of Time: Irish Evangelicals in the Age of Daniel O'Connell* (Montreal and Kingston: McGill-Queen's University Press, 2016); and for the spread of Darbyite Dispensationalism to the United States, see Akenson, *Exploring the Rapture: John Nelson Darby and the Victorian Conquest of North American Evangelicalism* (Oxford: Oxford University Press, 2018). Darby was originally an Anglican clergyman in the Church of Ireland.

113 An example of this occurred at the Central Committee meeting of the World Council of Churches in June 2016, in which a statement was approved that called on 'WCC member churches, specialized ministries and ecumenical partners ... to recognize Christian Zionism as a form of Christian fundamentalism'; available at www.oikoumene.org/en/resources/documents/central-committee/2016/statement-on-the-israeli-palestinian-conflict-and-peace-process (accessed 16/04/2019).

114 Gavin D'Costa, 'Search for the Promised Land', *The Tablet*, 3 March 2018, pp. 8–9; Dr Rowan Williams, Lecture to the 5th International Sabeel Conference 'Holy Land and Holy People' in Jerusalem, available at http://aoc2013.brix.fatbeehive.com/articles.php/1840/lecture-to-the-5th-international-sabeel-conference-holy-land-and-holy-people-jerusalem (accessed 16/04/2019). Dr Williams' lecture was dismissed at the time by Rosemary Radford Ruether, another participant at the conference, as 'an example of [the] more sophisticated and unconscious Christian Zionism in the established churches'.

115 The key figures in the development of Palestinian Christian liberation theology are Naim Ateek (Anglican), Geries Khoury (Melkite) and Mitri Raheb (Lutheran).

116 The Kairos Palestine document, titled *A Moment of Truth: A Word of Faith, Hope and Love from the Heart of Palestinian Suffering* (2009) can be read at www.kairospalestine.ps/index.php/about-us/kairos-palestine-document (accessed 16/04/2019).

117 There are a variety of conventions as to how to refer to the current social and political entities in what Christian tradition sometimes calls the Holy Land. This text follows the usage of e.g. the WCC in referring to 'Israel and Palestine'. Others would prefer to use 'Israel/Palestine'. The Foreign and Commonwealth Office speaks of 'Israel and the Occupied Palestinian Territories'. The choice of terminology is not intended to convey a particular position regarding either claims to territory or national self-understanding on the part of those currently living in the Holy Land.

118 National Jewish Scholars Project, *Dabru Emet: A Jewish Statement on Christians And Christianity* (2002), available at www.jcrelations.net/Dabru_Emet_-_A_Jewish_Statement_on_Christians_and_Christianity.2395.0.html (accessed 16/04/2019).

119 Quoted by Clare Amos in *Peace-ing Together Jerusalem* (Geneva: WCC, 2014), p. 97.

120 World Council of Churches Central Committee 1974.

121 *Land of Promise?* §§7.30–39; the final phrase is from *Kairos Palestine* §1.1.8. See also Amos, *Peace-ing Together Jerusalem*.

122 The range of Christian voices responsible for the *Kairos Palestine* document include several from the Eastern Christian tradition, both Orthodox and Catholic. It is salutary to remember that the repudiation of supersessionism which has been so important a development among Roman Catholic and liberal Protestant Churches over the last 50 years has not been extensively reflected in Eastern and Oriental Orthodox Churches. On supersessionism, see page 19 above.

123 The report *Zionism Unsettled* produced by the Israel/Palestine Mission Network of the Presbyterian Church, USA (2012) states categorically that 'The fundamental assumption of this study is that no exceptionalist claims can be justified in our interconnected pluralistic world.' The Presbyterian Church (USA) declined, however, to recognize this document as representing its view.

124 It is interesting to note that the Christian scholar Walter Brueggemann, in writing approvingly of the work of Mark Bravermann, a Jewish theologian who argues against the concept of 'chosenness', goes on to suggest that Christians too may need to revisit their own theological vocabulary of chosenness, in the Christian context focused on the uniqueness of Christ: see his Introduction to Mark Braverman, *Christians, Jews and the Search for Peace in the Holy Land* (Austin, TX: Synergy Books, 2010), pp. xv–

xvi. The corollary of Brueggemann's argument might be that if Christians wish to hold on a doctrine of the uniqueness of Christ, they also need to be willing to allow Judaism its own 'particularities'.

125 Quoted in Geoffrey Wigoder, *Jewish–Christian Relations since the Second World War* (Manchester: Manchester University Press, 1988), p. 109.

126 Cf. Moshe Halbertal, *People of the Book: Canon, Meaning and Authority* (Cambridge, MA: Harvard University Press, 1997).

127 Bernard Jackson, 'Legalism' *Journal of Jewish Studies* 30:1 (Spring 1979), pp. 1–22.

128 *The Way of Dialogue*, 'The Way of Hope', section 3.

129 Churches' Commission for Inter Faith Relations, *Christians and Jews,* p. 13.

130 *Sharing One Hope?,* p. 22.

131 National Jewish Scholars Project, *Dabru Emet.*

132 Compare on this point the document from the Conference of European Rabbis, Chief Rabbinate of Israel and Rabbinical Council of America, *Between Jerusalem and Rome: Reflections on 50 Years of Nostra Aetate (*2017), available at www.ccjr.us/dialogika-resources/documents-and-statements/jewish/cer-cri-rca-2017 (accessed 16/04/2019).

133 See the website for 'Pilgrim: A Course for the Christian Journey' at www.pilgrim course.org/. The commandments are ordered somewhat differently in Jewish and Christian tradition.

134 E.g. Commission for Religious Relations with the Jews, *Guidelines and Suggestions for Implementing the Conciliar Declaration* Nostra Aetate (no. 4) (1974), section IV, available at www.vatican.va/roman_curia/pontifical_councils/chrstuni/relations-jews-docs/rc_pc_chrstuni_doc_19741201_nostra-aetate_en.html (accessed 16/04/2019); *Notes on the Correct Way*, e.g. III.2 on Jesus and the Law.

135 See also Conference of European Rabbis, Chief Rabbinate of Israel and Rabbinical Council of America, *Between Jerusalem and Rome,* which notes that 'Despite profound theological differences, Catholics and Jews share common beliefs in the Divine origin of the Torah.'

136 Welby, 'Vigilance and Resolution', p. 11.

137 Rowan Williams: 'Auschwitz–Birkenau', 2008, available at http://aoc2013.brix. fatbeehive.com/articles.php/1026/auschwitz-birkenau (accessed 16/04/2019).

138 Williams, 'Auschwitz – Birkenau', 2008.

139 On the balance sought between liberty and order in Anglican tradition, see also the Anglican Communion Network for Interfaith Concerns, *Generous Love*, p. 4, where note 11 comments on the relationship between Pentecost in Christian tradition as a feast of the Holy Spirit and Shavuot in Jewish tradition as a festival focused on the giving of the Torah.

140 See e.g. David Novak, 'Maimonides and Aquinas on Natural Law', in *Talking with Christians: Musings of a Jewish Theologian* (Grand Rapids: Eerdmans, 2005), pp. 67–88.

141 This position is strongly supported in the final chapter of Justin Welby, *Reimagining Britain: Foundations for Hope* (London: Bloomsbury, 2018), titled 'The Churches and Other Faith Groups: Healthy Disruptors', pp. 253–70.